Don't like to read?
Just read the darker print for the main points!

UNMASKING BULLIES & VICTIMS

A Guide to Their Physiological, Psychological, and Emotional Patterns

By

Mary Louise Blakely

For Adolescents, Parents, Teachers, Bosses & Employees

Llumina Press

UNMASKING BULLIES & VICTIMS

A Guide to Their Physiological, Psychological, and

Emotional Patterns

BY

Mary Louise Blakely

Copyright 2004, Mary Louise Blakely

All rights reserved. No part of this publication may be reproduced or transmitted in any form or by any means electronic or mechanical, including photocopy, recording, or any information storage and retrieval system, without permission in writing from both the copyright owner and the publisher.

Requests for permission to make copies of any part of this work should be mailed to Permissions Department, Llumina Press, and PO BOX 772246, CORAL SPRINGS, FL 33077-2246.

ISBN: 1-932303-60-x
Printed in the United States of America

Library of Congress Cataloging-in-Publication Data

Blakely, Mary Louise.
  Unmasking bullies & victims : revealing their physiological,
psychological,   and emotional patterns / by Mary Louise Blakely.
      p. cm.
Includes bibliographical references and index.
  ISBN 1-932303-60-X (pbk. : alk. paper)
  1. Bullying. I. Title: Unmasking bullies and victims. II. Title.
  BF637.B85B56 2004
  302.3'4--dc21
                          2003012214

DEDICATION

This book is dedicated to all the bullies and victims who shared their life experiences with me and served as my teachers. You helped me to see the person behind the mask.

- To my family for your constant love and support.
- To my old and new friends for choosing to share life with me.
- To you, the reader, for choosing to read this book.
- To all of you who share this book with someone.
- To DS for the inspiration.

ACKNOWLEDGMENTS

I would like to acknowledge the contributions of those who helped make this book possible:

- My editor, Jan Andersen, who made sure that my written voice rings true.

- My son Chad, who painstakingly scrutinized and tweaked the manuscript in its early stages.

- Janet Illeni, for her suggestions and corrections.

- Llumina Press, for their guidance, patience, and support.

TABLE OF CONTENTS

UNMASKING BULLIES AND VICTIMS

Dedication

Acknowledgments

Preface   1

Introduction   3
    Who Are the Bully and the Victim?

Chapter One   9
    The Development of Four Bullies
        Bobby's Story   9
        Nancy's Story   11
        Jimmy's Story   12
        Tracy's Story   14

Chapter Two   19
    Bullies and Victims: How and Why

Chapter Three   25
    The Bully Mask
        Control and Fear   27
        Four Ways We Try to Control Others   27
        Fear, Bullies, and Victims   28

Chapter Four   33
    Beliefs & Experiences
        Beliefs and Judgments   35
        Beliefs and Loss   36

Chapter Five   41
    Four Reasons For Low Self-Esteem
        Poor Sensory Integration (SI)   42
        Homolateral Profiles   43
        Unaddressed Thinking Patterns   47
        Fear of Failure   49
        Putting It All Together   49

Chapter Six   55
    What You Know About the Person
    Behind the Mask
        Self-Assessment: Are You a Bully?   56

Chapter Seven   61
    The Bully's Victim
        Keeping Your Power   62
        The Victim Quiz: Do You Qualify?   66
        So, You Were Chosen to be the   66
        Victim. Now What?

Chapter Eight   71
    How to Stop Wearing the Mask
        Four Reasons People Choose to Fail   72
        Facing Fear   73
        Reconnecting With Ourselves   73
        Using Education to Heal   75

Chapter Nine   79
    The Adult Bully
        Dusting Off Our Childhood Masks   81

Chapter Ten   87
    What Do You Do With a Bully?
        For Students   88

For Parents	90
For Teachers	93
For Family and Friends	99
For Co-workers	100

Epilogue	105
Now That You Know!	

Appendices

Appendix 1 . . . Self-Esteem Builders	109
Appendix 2 . . . Quotes & Writings to Ponder	111
Appendix 3 . . . Letting Go	113
Appendix 4 . . . Helpful Multisensory Techniques for Teachers	115
Appendix 5 . . . Helpful Multisensory Techniques for Businesses	125
Appendix 6 . . . Exercise 1 – Identifying Your Beliefs	129
Appendix 7 . . . Exercise 2 – How Well Do You Nurture Yourself?	133
Appendix 8 . . . Exercise 3 – Identifying Close Energy-Takers	135
Appendix 9 . . . For Further Reading	139
Appendix 10 . . . The Restorative Justice Program	141
Appendix 11 . . . Other Publications by Mary Louise Blakely	143
Appendix 12 . . . Azuray Learning, Inc.	147

About the Author	151

PREFACE

In all areas of society there is a destructive dance taking place that I refer to as the "Bully & Victim Dance." It involves the bully and the bully's chosen dance partner, the victim. Over the years this dance has become increasingly popular and, as a result, fear, anger, and pain have become more prevalent in our homes, schools, workplaces, and global society.

> To stop the Bully & Victim Dance, we need to become emotionally literate. We have forgotten how to read and listen to our own, as well as our neighbor's, thoughts and feelings.

To become a healthier society, it is crucial for all of us to actively work toward this end. We can begin by teaching self-control and anger management classes that focus on interpersonal and intrapersonal communication skills in our schools and businesses.

Today, you can hear the following comments in any early elementary class on a playground:

"If I can't have it, you can't have it."
"I'm the best one and you're not."
"I had it first, so it's mine."
"You can't have it until I'm done with it."
"I don't like you if you don't like me."
"If you take mine, I'll take yours."

Unfortunately, similar childish conversations are taking place between nations in our global playgrounds among bullies who are trying to control who can play with what toy in which playground.

The bully and victim are among us and inside us. Every day more victims and bullies are born. It is my hope that this book will help you have a better understanding of why and how people become bullies and victims. *Unmasking Bullies and Victims* is not based on documented research. However, it does include the knowledge and insight I have gained through my years of work as an educator, learning/behavior specialist, and educational consultant within the educational and corporate arenas.

The information in these pages has already helped thousands of people to see the bigger picture behind their negative choices. I believe that we are all doing the very best we can to survive and grow, based upon the knowledge we have at any given moment in time. Sometimes we just need a safe place to regroup and gain more self-awareness. Please share this book with your friends, neighbors, students, co-workers, or family members, and give them the opportunity to discover the special and unique person they are.

INTRODUCTION

WHO ARE THE BULLY AND THE VICTIM?

You are probably reading this book for one of the following reasons:

- You are a bully.
- You are a bully's victim.
- You have been a bully or a victim.
- You want to be prepared to handle a bully.
- You believe that you are one of life's victims.
- You want to understand how and why bullying happens.

For a bully to exist, there needs to be a victim. This book offers adolescents and adults a quick-read approach to understanding the roles played in the Bully & Victim Dance. Considering our current nightly news reports, we all have a reason to better understand bullies and victims.

When you picture a bully or a victim, what type of person do you see? Do you picture a person who is strong, tall, and muscular? Do you see someone who is short and stocky, or thin and tall? Bullies and victims come in all shapes and sizes: tall, thin, short, fat, muscular, and flabby. They can be young or very old. Perhaps you see someone who threatens you or yells at you. Maybe you see someone who belittles you or hits you. Do you also picture someone who is charming yet manipulative, or generous and controlling? Perhaps you see yourself?

At the most basic level, bullies and victims are just people who are afraid of "not being enough." We all experience the feeling of not being enough any time we feel like we're less than another person – when we feel unloved, neglected, ugly, stupid, left out, or forgotten. These feelings can lead us to believe that we are incapable of being who we want to be or of having what we need to survive. This type of thinking may lead to a destructive belief, such as, "No matter what I do, I will never be or have enough." The belief that we are powerless can serve as a self-fulfilling prophecy that blocks us from creating successful experiences.

Believing they are powerless, some people choose to use aggressive or passive-aggressive techniques to manipulate others in order to gain power and control. These people are known as bullies and victims. **Bullies and victims are actually both power-takers and controllers who share the same belief of not being "enough."** The difference between the two is simple.

- *Bullies* believe that, in order to survive, people need to fight back and control others by using physical or emotional abuse. Bullies are aggressive controllers.

- *Victims* believe that, in order to survive, people need to give themselves away and depend on stronger individuals to save them. Victims are passive-aggressive controllers.

Bullies are people who believe they are powerless: they overtly <u>take</u> power from other people. Victims are people who believe they are powerless: they take power by appearing to give their power to other people.

The following chapters lead you through a simple, step-by-step process to help you understand how and why a person becomes a bully or a victim. You will learn the techniques needed to help you disarm the bully and truly empower the victim. You will also have the opportunity to understand yourself and the role you may be playing in the Bully & Victim Dance. Since anyone can be caught up in this dance, it is important for all of us to have the tools and knowledge presented in the following chapters.

Both bullies and victims are controllers. However, since the bully uses the most aggressive and painful power-taking techniques to control other people, the majority of this book is focused on the bully. As you continue to read about the bully, keep in mind that people who become bullies often start out with the belief that they are one of life's victims.

Chapter One presents brief case histories of four bullies, beginning with their early childhood and continuing into their lives as adults. The four histories include the most common traits that apply to bullies and victims I have worked with. By reviewing their stories, you can better understand how and why people become bullies or victims.

> ➤ **If you wish to skip the case histories and focus on the physical and mental creation of a bully, turn to Chapter Three. However, you might recognize someone you know in the next two chapters!**

Keep away from people who try to belittle your ambitions. Small people always do that, but the really great make you feel that you too can become great.

Mark Twain

CHAPTER ONE

THE DEVELOPMENT OF FOUR BULLIES

To understand how and why a person becomes a bully, it is helpful to explore the common childhood experiences that can contribute to the creation of a bully. This chapter presents case histories for Bobby, Nancy, Jimmy, and Tracy. They are all bullies.

Bobby's Story

Bobby appears to be a happy eight-year-old boy living with his mom and dad. He's a member of the T-Birds soccer team and he loves to play basketball. Bobby struggles in reading and math. He loves to play sports and would rather be outside instead of sitting still in a chair trying to read a book. Bobby learns best by touching and experiencing his environment through his muscles. It takes a lot of effort for Bobby to recall what he reads unless he has time to reread the words.

Because it takes him too long to fill in the answers, Bobby doesn't like to do worksheets. His hand and pencil just don't seem to work together. Bobby is smart enough to know that he's in the lowest reading group. (Kids always know which reading group is the lowest.) It isn't that Bobby can't read. He just has to reread everything in order to remember the information.

Bobby hasn't told anyone yet, but deep inside he believes there's something wrong with his brain. His friends don't have to work as hard as he does, and he always has to stay inside during recess to finish his work. At the end of the school day, Bobby can't wait to play soccer or basketball.

Most of the time, Bobby is happy. Even though he doesn't think he's smart in school, he knows that he's great at sports, so it's okay. Bobby really enjoys it when his dad shoots baskets with him. He also loves to show off his skills when his parents come to watch him play soccer. At eight years old, Bobby seems to be happy, even though school can be hard for him.

Three years later . . .

Bobby, now called Bob, is in sixth grade and his life has changed drastically. Bob is outside, shooting baskets by himself. It's a weekday, but he is home because he slugged a boy in school yesterday. Since he was already serving several detentions for fighting on the bus, Bob has been suspended from school until next week.

Bob is still struggling in school and he's flunking most of his classes. He just doesn't care about school. Because his mom and dad are divorced now, he isn't able to play soccer anymore. His dad lives too far away to take him to practice, and his mom would have to take time off from work.

Two years ago Bob had to move with his mom to an apartment. When he went to his new school, he tried to make new friends. He met his only two friends in detention, where they were sent after school for picking on and hurting other kids.

Bob is now wearing a "bully mask."

Years later . . .

Bob is now the owner of his own trucking company. He's a very hard boss to work for and he doesn't let anyone "run" him. He ended up dropping out of school in the ninth grade, but went back and got his GED several years later. Bob is a twice-divorced father of four children whom he "loves with a very heavy hand." He's been brought up on charges of abuse twice by one of his ex-wives, but the charges were dropped. He was also fired from being a coach for his son's soccer team due to inappropriate behavior, belittling his players.

Nancy's Story

Nancy is a third-grader who loves to draw and color. She likes school, except for the times when she gets yelled at for not paying attention. Her mother and her teacher are always telling Nancy that she doesn't listen. She does listen, but for some reason her brain can't remember what people say. It's especially hard for her to sit and listen when her teacher stands in front of the classroom and talks a lot.

Nancy is very good at drawing cartoons, and she likes to write creative stories about animals. Sometimes she thinks of stories in her mind when the teacher talks too long.

Nancy lives with her mom and stepfather. She's a happy girl who seems to have adjusted to living alternately with her mom and her biological dad, going back and forth every couple of weeks. Her dad is always covering his refrigerator with the pictures she draws for him. Nancy is very excited because her mom says she might let her take an art class downtown.

Two years later . . .

Nancy is now in fifth grade. Her mom and stepfather had a new baby eight months ago. At first, Nancy was thrilled with her baby sister. Then she discovered that nobody paid attention to her anymore. Two years ago, her dad married a woman with two daughters. One of the daughters is the same age as Nancy. Now Nancy spends only one day a month with her dad, and his refrigerator is covered with all three of his daughters' pictures.

Since Nancy's grades keep dropping, her mom hasn't let her attend any art classes downtown. Also, she isn't turning in her homework and she only has a few friends at school. Nancy is loud and gets into a lot of "girl fights" during recess. She thinks the principal, Mrs. Stone, has it in for her and likes to give her detention for fighting. Nancy's favorite comment is, "So why do I care?" She likes to dominate the other girls when she can get away with it. The teachers have nicknamed her "Queeny." When Nancy comes to class, she assumes her normal classroom pose by laying her head on her arms and closing her eyes. She just doesn't care. Her classmates know Nancy as a bully.

Years later . . .

Nancy's life spiraled downward in ninth grade when she was caught taking drugs. She also became pregnant and had to quit school to take care of her child. Because of her aunt's intervention, Nancy was able to turn her life around, graduate from another high school, and attend college. She graduated with a degree in marketing and is now working for a large marketing agency. Her co-workers see Nancy as a loner who doesn't let anyone get too close. She has a hard time taking any criticism and has been known to belittle co-workers when they suggest any changes be made to her work.

Jimmy's Story

Jimmy is a fourth-grader who loves to play hockey. His

father is a lawyer and his mom is a full-time homemaker. Jimmy's whole family loves the game of hockey. His older brother plays hockey, and he is one of the best players on the team. Jimmy loves the game, but he just wants to have fun on the ice. He's really not a competitor like his older brother. Jimmy also enjoys spending time with his grandpa.

School is easy for Jimmy and he works hard to make his parents proud of him. But lately, Jimmy's dad seems to be more focused on hockey scores than grades. His dad wants him to play hockey more aggressively and "think tough." To Jimmy, it seems like he can never please his dad. No matter how much he tries, it never seems to be enough. His dad always yells at him, telling him to toughen up and "be a man!" He forces Jimmy to work out with him in the basement every night before he goes to bed in order to, as his dad says, work on his "no-pain, no-gain attitude." Jimmy worries a lot, has stomachaches and nightmares, and bites his nails.

Three years later . . .

Jimmy is now known as "J.K." and is in seventh grade. His hair is longer and he wears an earring. His grandpa, the only one who really understood him, passed away a year ago. J.K.'s grades are low because he doesn't do his homework. "Not working up to his potential," "behavior problem," and "poor attitude" are always checked on his report card. Ever since J.K. quit hockey, his dad has ignored him or belittled him by calling him a "mama's boy."

But J.K. has learned how to be tough. He stands up to authority and often struts down the hallway yelling back "tough-guy" words when he's sent to the principal's office. J.K. calls everything "stupid" and makes fun of kids who aren't as smart as he is. He thinks all "hockey heads" are losers.

J.K. is known around school as a bully.

Years later . . .

In high school, J.K. decided to apply himself to his studies and use his brains to control people. After graduation, he went to college to become a lawyer. J.K. moved to the East Coast, where he is now a highly paid lawyer who is known as one of the cut-throat attorneys in his city. He's often quoted as saying, "no pain, no gain!" to his clients. He uses devious means to win his cases, and he believes that the end justifies the means. J.K. is a divorced father with one son. He's not very close to his boy; he says, "I'm just not the fatherly type."

Tracy's Story

Tracy is in fourth grade and is large for her age. She lives alone with her mom, who never married her dad. Tracy has only a few memories of her dad pushing her in a swing at some park when she was three or four years old. Tracy likes school, but math can be hard for her. She likes her teacher, Mrs. Welch, because she makes learning fun and lets Tracy use her fingers to count. Tracy is a happy girl who loves to sing, dance, and play with her puppy. She dreams of being a ballerina.

Two years later . . .

Tracy is now a sixth-grader. She towers over most of the other girls and boys in her class. She still loves to sing and dance, but only when she's alone. Over the years her classmates have teased her about her size and called her terrible names. Tracy doesn't turn in her homework and she daydreams in class a lot.

Tracy's mom has a live-in boyfriend now whom Tracy doesn't like. She can't tell her mom what he's really like or how badly he treats her when she's alone with him. She tried to tell her once, but her mom said Tracy made it up and didn't want to hear it. So Tracy has learned that, to survive in life, she can't trust anyone to take care of her except herself.

Tracy has been caught shoplifting and has been starting fights with the younger girls during recess. She has become very angry and mouthy toward her classmates. Tracy says she doesn't care about anybody or anything and yells, "Get out of my face" whenever someone tries to help her. Tracy intimidates the other girls – especially the younger ones – by threatening to hurt them. Because of her size, many girls are afraid of Tracy.

Tracy is known as a bully.

Years later . . .

Tracy is now a young, unwed mother who works on an assembly line in a large factory. She has been fired from several previous jobs due to her poor attitude and her inability to get along with her supervisors and co-workers. She became a drug user with two young children to support, so now she is working under a special government rehabilitation program for young mothers.

All four of these children started out with hopes, dreams, and joy in their lives. They were normal children, experiencing and enjoying life. All four became known as bullies by elementary or junior high school and have continued to bully others well into their adult lives.

Bobby, Nancy, Jimmy, and Tracy have stories that are similar to those of so many other individuals I have worked with. Although their stories and experiences appear to be different, they all have a lot in common. More about that in the next chapter.

It's not what happens to you, it's what you do about it.

W. Mitchell

CHAPTER TWO

BULLIES AND VICTIMS: HOW AND WHY

Let's take the information from the four case histories in the previous chapter and add it up to see if we can discover how and why a person becomes a bully.

All four of the children had several things in common early in their lives.

- Each of them appeared to be happy.

- Each of them was loved by an adult who was important to them.

- Most of them had some difficulty learning in school.

- They each had someone or something they felt good about, but they each also had an unresolved problem:

  - Bob had his mom and dad's love, and he loved playing soccer and basketball. He struggled with reading.
  - Nancy had her mom and dad's love, and she loved to draw. She struggled with sitting still and listening in school.
  - Jim had his grandfather's unconditional love, and he loved hockey. He felt he could never please his parents – especially his dad.
  - Tracy had her mother's love, and she loved to sing and dance. Math and reading were hard for her. Her classmates teased her about her size.

Later in their lives they all had the same thing in common. **All four of them were forced to give up – or they lost – the parts of their lives that they enjoyed and felt good about. They did not replace this loss with something positive.**

Bob lost:
- His family unit
- Time with his dad
- His old school friends
- His ability to play soccer
- His self-esteem

Nancy lost:
- Her place in both families
- Time with her dad
- The opportunity to take art classes
- Her self-esteem

Jim lost:
- His grandpa
- His desire to play hockey
- His desire to achieve
- His self-esteem

Tracy lost:
- Her feelings of love and security
- Her passion for singing and dancing
- Her desire to care about her life
- Her self-esteem

They all shared the following common beliefs about not being enough and not having control:

- No matter what I do, I will never be good enough.

- I'm the only one I can count on to survive.
- Nothing good lasts.
- I can never have what I want.

Many negative childhood experiences can lead us to have victim-based beliefs about ourselves. These beliefs can cause us to make negative choices that keep us from succeeding. They can also serve as the triggers for our minds and bodies to begin creating a "bully mask." The next chapter explains how important the mind and body connection is in the creation of this mask and introduces the main ingredient behind the mask.

You gain strength, courage, and confidence by every experience in which you really stop to look fear in the face. You are able to say to yourself, "I lived through this horror. I can take the next thing that comes along." You must do the thing you think you cannot do.

Eleanor Roosevelt

CHAPTER THREE

THE BULLY MASK

The Creation of the Bully Mask

The main ingredient for the creation of a "bully mask" is fear. Fear is a trigger that can cause our minds and bodies to start the process of creating the mask. It all begins with our reaction to a fear that is connected to a negative belief.

At the base or lower section of our brain is what is called the "primitive brain" or "reactive brain." This part of the brain is similar to that of a rat or raccoon. Its main purpose is to keep us alive. Whenever a raccoon or a rat feels like it is in danger, it tries to escape or fight in order to survive. This is known as the "fight or flight" response.

From the reactive brain's point of view, human beings respond just like a rat or a raccoon when we believe we are in danger. It doesn't matter to our reactive brain if a tiger is chasing us, a teacher is calling on us to answer a question, or a boss is demanding an immediate verbal account of a project. If we believe we aren't fast enough to outrun that tiger, smart enough to know the answer to a teacher's question, or prepared enough to supply the report to a boss, our reactive brain kicks us into "fight or flight." That's when our hearts beat faster, our stomachs churn, our hands get clammy, and our throats have lumps. The reactive brain is now in charge, and it is preparing us to fight back or escape from a threatening situation.

Whenever we fear loss of control in our lives, we go into a fight or flight pattern. We may not actually *be* in danger, but we are afraid that in some way we aren't enough: not smart enough, not brave enough, or not attractive enough. To our reactive brain, this fear means, "I might not survive!"

The following information is an excerpt from the author's book, *Why Not You?*

> "…To keep your reactive brain from controlling you, you simply need to acknowledge your fear. Once you say to yourself (silently or out loud) 'I'm afraid,' your primitive/reactive brain has done its job. It raised the alarm and prepared your body to react.
>
> Now your higher brain functions can take over, and things will start to settle. Your heartbeat and breathing will slow down, and your blood pressure will fall.

Once this happens, you can choose how to respond to a threatening situation. As long as you are being controlled by your body's reactions, you are no different than an animal living on its survival instinct. Yet, by acknowledging your fear and using your higher brain functions to deal with what is occurring, you can choose to fight, flee, or understand and face your fear. ..."

Control and Fear

The more we feel threatened, the more we fear loss of control. And the more we fear loss of control, the more we try to control other people to regain our own sense of well-being. This happens when we are in a reactive state, when we allow our anger and fear to control us.

Of course, we all experience feeling angry at certain times. However, did you know that **anger is always based on a fear of not being "enough"?**

Four Ways We Try to Control Others

Here are four techniques humans use to try to control one another whenever they experience fear.

- Using physical or emotional abuse (most aggressive)
- Verbally belittling or intimidating others (aggressive)
- Shutting people out or putting up a wall (passive-aggressive)
- Making others feel sorry or guilty (least passive-aggressive)

The most aggressive of these four are the top two: physical/emotional abuse and belittling/intimidating others. Bullies who use these techniques directly attack you and take your energy by threatening you and trying to make you think like them.

Less overtly aggressive, yet still powerful, are the passive-aggressive techniques at bottom of the list. These tend to be used by passive-aggressive energy-takers who believe that they are victims. They are the martyrs and shielders who emotionally seduce you into helping them. You can never do enough for those who use the bottom two methods of control. They use guilt to make you believe that (1) you are the reason for their anger/failure, or (2) they will fail without you.

The bottom line is that **all four of these control techniques are used in an attempt to take away another person's power and control and gain it for ourselves.** Each of us has our two favorite control techniques that we learned from our parents or the influential adults in our lives. They, in turn, learned these control techniques from their parents or the adults who influenced them. Unconsciously, we pass on our survival techniques to our children.

Fear, Bullies, and Victims

We have all probably been bullies to some degree and may even become bullies again. Whenever we fear that we aren't enough, we become angry. Strong anger reflects a lot of pain and great fear of not being enough. The deeper the fear or pain a bully carries inside, the greater the pain a bully inflicts on others.

> **The amount of pain a person carries inside may be reflected in the amount of pain that person causes others in the outside world.**

Many birds, insects, and animals have a way of looking, sounding, or acting scary in order to protect and mask themselves from predators. We humans also wear many masks in an effort to feel safe. We try to look, act, and talk like we're big, smart, tough, and strong. **The more we "strut our stuff" and act like we don't care, the more we reveal how much we really *do* care.**

Instead of acting big, smart, tough, and strong, some people choose to feel safe by taking on the passive victim role. They play the part of a possum by numbing out ("playing dead"). Or they act like a turtle, going into their shells and putting up a shield.

Whether they use an aggressive or passive-aggressive approach, behind every mask is a scared person who believes that he or she isn't good enough. No matter how big or old the person behind the mask is, that person is afraid. When people shout at, hit, kick, tease, manipulate, or hurt others, they are feeling powerless. To feel safe, they want to take your power or control away from you.

People who are actually in control of themselves are empowered. They know that they are enough. They don't need to take power from other people to feel okay about themselves.

We all want to have some control in the following areas:

- All people want to survive.
- All people want to be safe.
- All people want to be healthy.

- All people want to feel and express love.
- All people want to have their hopes, dreams, and passions fulfilled.
- All people want to know that they are enough.

When we believe we have some control, we can manage our lives better and feel good about ourselves. Yet when we focus on our fear of losing control, we usually experience loss in that area. As a result, we begin to buy into a victim's mindset – all based on a belief of never having or being enough.

"No matter what I do, I will never be good enough" is a common belief in both bullies and victims. Here are some other typical negative belief statements:

- "If you're looking for someone to mess up, I'm the one."
- "It seems like no matter what I do, it's never good enough."
- "I'll never be able to show anyone what I can do. It's like my brain just shuts down when I try to show them."
- "There's something wrong with my brain. I'm just stupid."
- "I must be retarded. They put me in Special Ed."

In the next two chapters you will learn more about why people start to believe that they aren't "good enough" at an early age.

I would not waste my life in friction
when it could be turned into momentum.
                                                Frances Willard

CHAPTER FOUR

BELIEFS AND EXPERIENCES

You Experience What You Believe

What you believe inside, you experience as you function in the world. Ironically, the bully and the victim often share a similar life experience because they are operating out of the same belief based on fear: both of them believe they are not "good enough." This belief can cause them to continually attract negative experiences into their lives in order to support their beliefs.

For example:

- If you believe that nobody likes you, you will experience having no friends.

- If you believe that you never get what you want, your experiences will focus on always pleasing others and leaving yourself out.

- If you believe that the other guy always gets what he wants and that you'll never have what *you* want, you will block your own progress.

Many people sabotage their opportunities in life by setting themselves up to give away what they really want. As a result, they continually feed their belief of not being good enough or worthy enough to receive.

> Until you see the connections between your beliefs and your experiences, you will always see yourself as a victim.

Bullies are usually people who believe they can't trust life. Believing that they are life's victims who need to take control in order to be safe, they look for weaker victims to dominate. Only people who believe deep inside that they're powerless need to work so hard to feel powerful.

However, when power-takers know and understand the truth behind their actions, they can uncover their negative beliefs and change them into positive beliefs. For example, "My life is a mess" can become "I am in the process of changing my life." And "I can never have what I want" can become "I create a life that is full of wonderful opportunities."

It doesn't matter if our beliefs are positive or negative; we always feed our beliefs. This tendency is so strong that we'll even try to convince others that our negative beliefs about ourselves are right!

"See, I told you I couldn't do it," and "See, I told you I'd mess up," are statements based on the belief "I'm a failure." If we change our negative belief, we can change our experiences.

> Behind every pattern of negative experiences is a negative belief being fed by YOU!

Beliefs and Judgments

Where do we get our negative beliefs? Let's say you're part of an audience. Someone asks everyone who can sing to raise their hand. Would you do it? Many of us who believe we aren't "good enough" singers might keep our hands in our laps.

But we all *can* sing – that is, we are physically able to sing if we have vocal chords. But because of a judgment made by a family member, friend, or someone else to whom we gave authority, we may have bought into the belief, "I'm not a good singer."

We've all bought into many negative beliefs about ourselves that we aren't even aware of. As a result, we're supporting our unknown, negative judgments almost every minute of every day. Listen to your inner thoughts. Are they always positive? If you ever start a thought with "I'll never ..." or "I can't ...," try to discover the negative belief behind that thought.

What might be the negative beliefs behind the following statements?

"I'll never be a good reader."
"It never seems to work out for me."
"I can't play because I'm too slow."
"I'll never_____." (You finish this one!)

Look at your negative experiences that seem to have a repetitive pattern in your life, and see if you can recognize the belief(s) behind the pattern. You might be carrying a negative belief that you're unconsciously feeding.

(To help identify your negative beliefs, turn to "Identifying Your Beliefs," Exercise 1, Appendix 6 at the back of the book.)

Beliefs and Loss

Life is a continuous process of growing up, and growing up involves the process of letting go. The more we advance through life, the more we have to let go. The process of letting go comes with the loss of a friend, a divorce, a move, the loss of a job, the death of a loved one, or just a change in daily routine. **When we believe that a person or thing is vital to our survival, we fear that we might not survive without him, her, or it.** Because we fear loss, we want to keep things the same and be in control.

> Many people reject change in their lives because they fear giving up control. The unknown is very scary to a person who fears any loss of control.

Sometimes our fear of losing control is so great that we feel driven to *always* have control.
If we believe that we won't experience emotional or physical pain again if we always have control, we can become consumed with a desperate need to control our environment and the people in it.

This need to be in control all the time takes a lot of energy.

Our fear of losing control of our lives can cause us to become day-to-day survivors on a treadmill that never goes anywhere. Focusing on trying to make it safely through each day, while carrying around all that fear, robs us of a lot of our own energy.

When we focus on just surviving every day, our hopes, dreams, and passions are often buried. Once we get caught up in this "survivor mode," we can easily become a bully or a victim. However, when we finally realize that we can survive loss in many areas of life, we become stronger from the experience and begin to hope and dream again.

People participate in many dysfunctional dances in order to be loved and feel safe. In any dysfunctional situation, there is a control dance in which many people are involved. Now that you are aware of this, observe the control techniques you and others use. What fears are being fed? What control techniques are being used? What does each person gain by using one of the four control techniques? By understanding instead of judging the person behind the mask – whether it's you or another person – you can choose to change the "dance."

The next chapter presents four reasons children come to believe and feel they aren't good enough. These early feelings and beliefs are very painful and often carry over into adulthood. They can become the catalyst for the creation of a bully or victim mask.

Be kind, for everyone you meet is fighting a battle.

Plato

CHAPTER FIVE

FOUR REASONS FOR LOW SELF-ESTEEM

People experience many losses in their lives, such as losing a parent, a job, or a home. Losing your belief in yourself when you're young can have a devastating effect on the rest of your life. It can keep your passion and potential buried under the fear of never being good enough.

Below is a list of the concerns parents express when their children are having problems:

- Anger
- Depression
- Lying
- Acting out or fighting
- Lack of focus
- Poor coordination
- Nightmares
- Stomachaches
- Eating problems
- Low grades
- Not doing homework
- Not turning in homework
- Reading, math, and writing problems

Almost all of these problems are connected in some way to low self-esteem that is based on the fear of not being good enough.

I believe there are four primary reasons many elementary school children start to develop low self-esteem:

1. Poor sensory integration
2. Homolateral profiles
3. Unaddressed thinking patterns
4. Fear of failure

Poor Sensory Integration (SI)

Sensory integration, or SI, is the ability of both hemispheres of the brain to communicate with each other. SI is necessary for optimal learning. Some children start school before they have all of their senses integrated correctly. Children who have incomplete sensory integration are often considered to be clumsy or even dyslexic. For example, they may exhibit sloppy handwriting, appear to be uncoordinated, write with reversed letters, or scrunch all their letters together in the margins on their paper. **Sensory integration usually takes place naturally when a child crawls, because crawling involves integrating both sides of the body.**

There can be many different reasons for poor SI. But for children who are not sensory-integrated the result is the same: they struggle in the learning process. Over time they might begin to believe that learning is hard and that they aren't as smart as their peers.

How do you know if a child has poor sensory integration? One easy screen for incomplete SI is poor eye tracking. It is important for all young children to be checked to see if their eyes track moving objects together. Here's a quick check. Hold a pencil in front of the child's eyes. Now move the pencil from side to side and up and down in front of the child's face. Watch to see if both eyes work together and track the moving pencil correctly. Another simple way to check for sensory integration is to see if a six-year-old child can skip.

There are several activities and exercises children can do to become more sensory-integrated. Swimming, tennis, juggling scarves, pushing a small ball across the floor with the nose, hopscotch, gymnastics, and dancing are all excellent activities to improve a child's SI. Use activities that help children gain coordination by moving their arms or legs across their body simultaneously (e.g., marching in place while touching the left hand to the right knee, and visa versa.)

Homolateral Profiles

Our brains are divided down the middle, front to back, into two hemispheres. Most of us access and process information more effectively on one side of our brain than the other. The side of our brain that we use the most is known as our **dominant hemisphere**.

It is also important to know that, in most people, **the right side of the body is controlled by the left hemisphere of the brain, and the left side of the body is controlled by the right hemisphere of the brain.**

We learn best when the eye, ear, hand, and foot we favor the most are on the side *opposite that of our dominant hemisphere*. (In other words, when the dominant hemisphere of the brain is in control of the parts of our body that we are most comfortable using.) This is called a pure cross-lateral profile.

However, when a person's favored eye, ear, hand, and foot are on the *same side of the body as the dominant hemisphere*, the body is being controlled by the side of the brain that we use the least. This is called a pure homolateral profile.

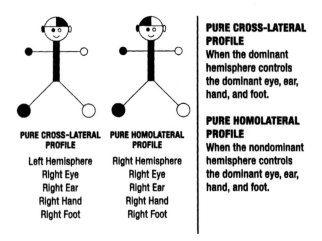

PURE CROSS-LATERAL PROFILE
When the dominant hemisphere controls the dominant eye, ear, hand, and foot.

PURE HOMOLATERAL PROFILE
When the nondominant hemisphere controls the dominant eye, ear, hand, and foot.

PURE CROSS-LATERAL PROFILE
Left Hemisphere
Right Eye
Right Ear
Right Hand
Right Foot

PURE HOMOLATERAL PROFILE
Right Hemisphere
Right Eye
Right Ear
Right Hand
Right Foot

There are many variations on the pure homolateral profile. For example, these are all partial homolateral profiles:

- If you have a dominant *right hemisphere*, prefer to write with your *right hand*, and tend to use your *right eye* more than your left

- If you have a dominant *right hemisphere*, prefer to use your *left hand*, and favor your *right eye*

- If you have a dominant *left hemisphere*, prefer to write with your *right hand*, and favor the use of your *left eye*

Why does all this matter? **When they are under stress, people with homolateral profiles struggle in some way with decreased learning efficiency.** In most situations, they can switch processing sensory information between brain hemispheres with no problem. However, under stress, information coming in from a dominant sense is limited because it is controlled by the hemisphere of the brain that is not dominant.

Unmasking Bullies   45

This is a brief introduction to the very complex topic of brain processing profiles. To understand the effect of a primarily homolateral profile in real life, here is Julie's story.

THE BLOCKED WRITER

Julie is a writer. Her brain is right-hemisphere dominant, she is right-handed, and her left eye is dominant. Her right ear and right foot are also dominant. Julie loves to write stories late at night when she's cozy and bundled up with a comforter around her. Her thoughts flow easily onto the paper as she becomes immersed in her story.

One day, Julie's English teacher decided to have her class take a timed essay test about a novel the class had been discussing. Since Julie is an excellent writer, she was thrilled to have a written test; she never did well on multiple choice tests.

But when it came time for Julie to begin her essay test, she felt like her thoughts were stuck in her head. Nothing seemed to flow. She just couldn't write down all the thoughts that she wanted to express. She kept crossing out her sentences and erasing her words. She became so nervous that she panicked. "Why can't I write my thoughts? I love to write!"

This is an example of how a homolateral profile can affect performance. Julie could write her thoughts down quickly when she was relaxed and could adjust her profile. But under stress, she became nervous.

Since her right hemisphere controls her dominant (left) eye and her left hemisphere controls her dominant (right) hand, the information from her dominant hand and dominant eye are not controlled by the same brain hemisphere. In Julie's case, the information coming into her system from her hand is slower to process over to her right hemisphere, which controls her eye.

It needs to be emphasized that **a person with a pure or partially homolateral profile will only be affected like this under stressful situations.** When students with a homolateral profile experience this stress (taking a timed test or writing an essay in class), they often find that their thoughts are blocked. They just can't recall what they studied. When they feel rushed or anxious, these students may erase their work a lot and even reverse letters in words. Because of this, many children who have homolateral profiles grow up believing they have something wrong with their brains.

Homolateral profiles have nothing to do with having a brain defect or being less intelligent. Many children with homolateral profiles buy into believing they are stupid when they can't remember the material they studied the night before. When they realize they can't recall the information, these children become even more stressed. Their fear of failing the test takes control, and they end up blocking their thoughts even more. Thus, they receive yet another low test score to add to their belief, "I always fail tests."

Children with this profile block their thoughts mostly due to stress and incorrect learning techniques. By teaching them how to imprint information into their minds for greater recall, they can have greater success in learning. For example, some techniques that seem to help homolateral learners increase their performance include these:

- Use a green transparency over visual work.
- Perform large muscle movements.
- Drink lots of water.
- Use color visualizations (i.e., imagine a certain color covering the papers while reading or writing).

Over the years, countless students with a homolateral profile have cried tears of relief after learning that they aren't stupid and that there isn't anything wrong with their brains. Many reveal for the first time their deepest fear: "My brain has something wrong with it." Usually, this secret has been eating away at their self-esteem for years. Having believed that, "No matter what I do, I will never be good enough," these children may create a mask. They may choose to become a bully, acting out their anger and frustration. Or they may choose to play the part of the victim and just give up.

Unaddressed Thinking Patterns

In the classroom, children are most often asked to *look at* and *listen to* what is being taught instead of getting up and experiencing the lesson using a hands-on approach. Therefore, for students who require hands-on learning experiences, learning can be very difficult.

Children who learn best through their sense of touch or movement are often forced to rely on their weaker senses by only hearing or seeing the information. As a result, many of these students zone out or daydream during class if they sit too long. Although they may perform well in science labs, gym class, and in group projects (and may excel in taking things apart, sports, dancing, or drawing), they will often feel frustrated if they have to depend on handouts, reading material, charts, and lectures for learning the information.

This group of students has difficulty learning in traditional classrooms where reading, writing, and lectures dominate. However, it isn't that they can't learn this way – they just need to work harder to imprint the information correctly into their minds by using movement, repetition, and other techniques that support their learning patterns.

Children who have a hard time recalling what they *see* usually have to reread written material in order to comprehend what it says. Since reading and writing can be harder for them, they often choose to turn in incomplete work or use the excuse of "I forgot" when asked about their books or homework. Because many of them cannot picture things in their mind without using their sense of touch or movement, cause and effect thinking is also another challenge for them.

Children who experience difficulty recalling what they *hear* must depend on repetition or movement for greater recall. They are often thought of as being lazy, shy, or daydreamers. Many have difficulty expressing their feelings and can be misunderstood or labeled unsociable by those who like to talk and share their thoughts. As a result of bottling up their emotions, these children often have tempers and stomachaches.

Many of these children grow up believing that they aren't smart and that learning is harder for them. Some of them will develop low self-esteem and decide to give up trying to learn. However, this can be avoided. **These children need to experience new information by interacting more with their learning environment.** If they are offered learning opportunities that combine visual and auditory information with touch and movement, they can learn the information much more easily.

Fear of Failure

To stop feeling dumb, slow, or stupid, many children try to escape the pain of repeated failure by shutting down and "choosing" not to study or do homework. They may even use the excuse, "I forgot" to avoid failure.

Too often, children who have a hard time recalling or focusing on what they *hear* are yelled at for not paying attention or listening. In reality, these children may remember for a very long time anything said to them in negative way. Therefore, because any corrective statement made by an adult can sound many times "louder" to these children, they learn to shield themselves by blocking out negative words. They become selective listeners.

Children who have a hard time recalling what they *see* are very sensitive to judgmental or angry looks. As a result, they will often avoid eye contact with others. Since these children become more easily discouraged with correction marks on their papers, many of them use the "out of sight, out of mind" approach to cope. They wad up their work, toss it away, or "lose" it.

Putting it All Together

When children struggle with learning or performance, they may develop a negative belief about who they are based on the judgments of other people. Children who are not fully sensory-integrated, who have homolateral profiles, or who learn best by touching and moving, are often negatively labeled and judged by adults and peers early in life. They may grow up believing that no matter what they do, they'll never be good enough. Because they are afraid they are not good enough to succeed, too many of them become bullies or victims. This fear can create very deep, painful feelings of shame and suffering that can influence their entire lives.

> **If we can address and positively deal with a child's negative beliefs early enough, we can begin to heal the wounded child and stop the creation of the bully mask.**

We can help children experience a healthy, happy childhood by becoming aware that there may be many reasons behind their low grades and negative actions. Adults tend to quickly judge, label, and punish children without thinking this through. Many of our most successful and talented people struggled daily in reading or math. (Albert Einstein was academically challenged and did poorly in school.)

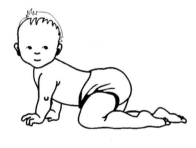

Perhaps we can all learn from the child that we once were by remembering a time when we weren't so quick to judge each of life's processes as a "success" or "failure." A baby doesn't believe he's a failure every time he falls down while he's trying to walk. Falling down is just part of the process of strengthening his legs. In fact, it is precisely because we all fell down repeatedly that we can walk!

Being able to risk failure in order to succeed involves knowing that we are strong enough to survive losing. In life's classroom, the best learning takes place when the learner knows that he or she can survive the risk of being wrong.

In the next chapter you will have the opportunity to see what you now know about the bully and the victim. Don't be surprised if you see yourself or someone you know!

If you don't have the power to change yourself,
then nothing will change around you.

Anwar Sadat

CHAPTER SIX

WHAT YOU KNOW ABOUT THE PERSON BEHIND THE MASK

Let's stop and review what you know about the bully and the victim.

Although this is a short chapter, it's one of the most important in this book. You will see how much you know about bullies and understand how to apply this information to the people in your life. Even more important, you can apply the information to yourself.

Every person is, has been, or will be a bully and/or a victim at some time in life. After you review the following bulleted information, read over the list on the next page titled, "Are You A Bully?" to see if you are currently wearing the bully mask.

- A bully is really a scared person who uses the attitude, "I'm tough" or "I don't care about you." This is designed to keep people at a distance or get victims to give away their power.

- Every time a person puts another person down, hurts others, or tries to use any of the four control techniques, that person is revealing how afraid he or she is behind the mask.

- People who hurt other people to feel powerful are really feeling powerless. They overpower their victims in an attempt to feel they have regained control.

55

- The greater their fear of being powerless (not "enough"), the more control/power bullies believe they need to have to survive.

- Bullies want to feel unconditionally loved and safe, and to know that they are enough.

- Bullies just want to regain the control they believe they have lost.

Self-Assessment: Are You a Bully?

- ❑ Do you take things or privileges away from others to control them?

- ❑ Do you physically abuse others when they stand up to you?

- ❑ Do you belittle others who don't agree with you?

- ❑ Do you lose your temper when you feel disrespected?

- ❑ Is it hard to allow others to tell you what to do?

- ❑ Do you believe that people will stab you in the back if you don't watch them?

- ❑ Do you drag your heels and keep others waiting for you?

- ❑ Are you sarcastic?

- ❑ Do you consider feedback from others to be unimportant?

- ❑ Do you frequently say, "I don't care what you think. My mind is made up."?

- ❑ Do you tell others how to think, act, look, feel, or behave?

- ❑ Are you deaf to the word "NO"?

If you answered yes to three or more of these questions, you may be a bully.

Now that you know, you can be more aware of your behavior. From now on, you have the potential to catch yourself in the process of putting on the bully mask before you actually decide to wear it.

In the next chapter we'll explore the bully's partner in the Bully & Victim Dance: the victim.

The best years of your life are the ones in which you decide your problems are your own. You don't blame them on your mother, the ecology, or the president. You realize that you control your own destiny.

Albert Ellis

CHAPTER SEVEN

THE BULLY'S VICTIM

Bullies are like hungry tigers, hunting down their weakest victims in order to feed their need for power and control. The more they fear being powerless, the more they crave power and control.

Whenever you feel that a person is trying to belittle you, physically or emotionally wound you, make you feel guilty, or treat you like you don't matter or exist, you have been selected to be the victim of a bully. You have been selected for *appearing* to be weak.

Some people believe that bullies do not feel powerless and that they really are arrogant and self-centered. I do not agree. **Bullies may appear to be arrogant because of the mask they wear, but the person behind that mask feels powerless.**

Why do people become self-centered and arrogant with the desire to hurt others? Because they need to believe they are stronger and more powerful than another to ease their fear of being powerless. They may look big, tough, and arrogant, but many bullies cry real tears of pain. It doesn't matter if they are children or adults; all bullies are just scared little boys and girls hiding behind big masks of fear. They all hunger for everything that empowers all of us: love, security, success, hopes, dreams, and passion for life.

Children and adults who are emotionally and physically tortured by bullies need to have strong emotional <u>support</u>, with swift, protective <u>action</u> taken on their behalf. Victims should not have to wait for their bruises to show before they receive help.

Businesses and schools need to have strict procedures and policies to deal with bullying. **For victims to feel safe enough to stand up to a bully or to a group of bullies, they need to have the strong support of family, friends, co-workers, administrators, and society.** Whenever people or institutions are blind and deaf to acts of victimization, the bully wins.

Keeping Your Power

Fear and anger are the tools the bully uses to push your buttons. The more you are angry or fearful, the more power the bully takes from you. Yet, **if you can remember that the person behind the mask feels powerless, you can maintain your perspective and not allow the bully to push your buttons.**

By acknowledging your anger without acting on it, you can stop yourself from joining the Bully & Victim Dance. Observe yourself feeling angry without having to "be" angry. Instead of saying, "I am angry" say, "I feel angry." There is a difference.

When you start to observe yourself *feeling* your anger before you *become* angry, you can learn to maintain your emotional balance and remain calm and level-headed. By keeping your head and staying in control of your emotions you can keep your power.

Although victims of bullies often believe they are weak and needy, it doesn't mean that every victimized person carries these beliefs. However, if people continue to draw more bullies and loss into their lives, they may be unknowingly feeding a belief based upon a fear of not being enough.

Some people are bullied because they are considered by the bully to be too nice to do anything to retaliate. These potential victims may also be selected because the bully is jealous of them. A bully will continue to torment and torture anyone who is seen as a threat or an easy target.

People who have been the target of a bully can carry a lot of shame. Feelings of hopelessness and defeat are usually mixed in with their anger. Sadly, some victims choose to end the emotional and physical pain inflicted on them by ending their own lives. As a result, we now have the term "bullicide" to refer to victims who commit suicide in order to end the pain of being bullied. Until our society decides to implement a zero-tolerance policy for bullies in our institutions, the Bully & Victim Dance will continue.

A TYPICAL VICTIM STORY

When I was a junior high school teacher, I had a boy in my math class who was bullied at the drinking fountain by several students every day during a break. Even with me or another teacher stepping in to intervene, the bullying persisted. To them, he was just the new boy that they could pick on – a fun diversion to help them look "cool" to their friends.

Finally I decided to use another approach to stop the bullying. Instead of admonishing the students, I decided to educate them with a dose of reality. I spoke with the young boy who was being bullied.

I asked him if he would like the opportunity to speak to the class about what it felt like to be bullied. I explained that I didn't think the students who bullied him really understood what it was like for him, and that speaking to them would be a good way to help them understand the pain they caused. He agreed to share his thoughts and feelings with the class by using me as his backup.

This boy believed he was one of life's victims. He had a lot of anger stuffed inside him. He was small, he stuttered, and he didn't wear the "in" clothes like the other kids – his parents couldn't afford to buy them. He had transferred from another school in order to start over and get away from the students who teased him there.

The day he stood in front of my classroom and spoke so courageously to his classmates was a turning point for him as well as the other students. Although his body shook and his stuttering increased when he started to talk, he was determined to share his thoughts with them. He finally had the chance to take control and express his pain.

He told them how he threw up every night and how he begged his mom to let him stay home every morning. He told them that he hated coming to school and that he had nightmares every night. He shared that in second grade he even tried to hang himself with a chain from his swing set because he just didn't want to live anymore. He even told them that there were days when he still didn't want to live.

After he was done speaking, the room was silent. The boys who had bullied him sat very still. Some of them had tears in their eyes. I asked my class if they'd like to say anything to him. All of the students raised their hands. They apologized and had supportive comments. From that day on, they treated him differently.

I wish I could add that he had more friends and wasn't bullied again. I can't. He still ate his lunch alone, and he still wasn't accepted enough to be invited to parties or to their homes. But I didn't see any students from my classroom tease him again, and I even overhead some of my students sticking up for him in front of some other bullies from another grade.

The Victim Quiz: Do You Qualify?

Check the list below and see if you have been, or are, a victim.

- ❑ Do you get hurt by a lot of people?
- ❑ Do you count on stronger people to save you or make you happy?
- ❑ Have you trusted people, only to be hurt by them later?
- ❑ Do you always have to please people?
- ❑ Do you worry about people judging you?
- ❑ Do you avoid conflicts?
- ❑ Do you think that bad things always happen to you?
- ❑ Do you believe that no matter what you do, it never works out?
- ❑ Do you enter a room expecting to be teased or bullied?
- ❑ Do you find yourself having to do everything for everyone?

If you answered "yes" to just one of these questions, you are primed and ready to be victimized by a bully.

So, You Were Chosen to Be the Victim. Now What?

Let's say you have demonstrated some victim-like behaviors. If there are bullies in the vicinity, they will know this and test you to see how weak you are. They will be aware that you easily give away your power when you are afraid.

So what do you do to keep from being bullied? The answer sounds simple, but it means that you must find the courage to take action. **When you choose to keep your power, the bully will find another victim.**

Unmasking Bullies

- Acknowledge that you have been selected to be the bully's victim for a reason.

- Identify what the bully gains by victimizing you. *Why* were you selected?

- Own your role as the chosen victim. (Until you do, you'll continue to feed your power to the bully.)

- Identify what you gain by choosing to be the victim. What belief are you feeding?

- Remember, you *don't* have to give your power away to be accepted, safe, or loved.

- Understand the bully's weakness. What need are you filling for the bully?

- Stand up for yourself. Take action to change the situation.

- Decide to keep your power:
    - Don't allow the bully to push your buttons.
    - Don't put yourself in front of the bully.
    - Don't antagonize the bully.
    - Ignore the bully.
    - Do not become your fear or anger.
    - Stay in control of your emotions. Try to observe yourself feeling your emotions rather than being angry or afraid.
    - Tell someone in authority. Don't be afraid to ask for help.

- Begin to believe in yourself. Stop putting yourself down.

The next chapter explains how both victims and bullies can stop wearing their masks, and discusses the steps involved in the unmasking process.

The game of life is the game of boomerangs. Our thoughts, deeds, and words return to us sooner or later, with astounding accuracy.

Florence Shinn

CHAPTER EIGHT

HOW TO STOP WEARING THE MASK

Let's review what you now know about bullies, victims, fear, and loss of control. Both bullies and victims need to understand that when they take someone's power or blame other people, they are feeling powerless. The more they fear the loss of control, the more controlling they try to become.

The feeling of losing control or feeling powerless always translates in the primitive/reactive mind to, "I may not survive." This is a core fear connected to the most basic needs of human nature.

The bully and/or victim can trigger inside us any time we believe that we aren't good enough or will never have enough. The more deeply we believe we aren't enough, the greater our fear of losing control and not being safe. As a result, the more we fear for our safety or fear loss, the more we believe we need to become controllers.

I met a wise woman whose friends and family had experienced much suffering at the hands of several violent groups during a war in her native country. Although she had witnessed and experienced deep loss from their actions, she shared great wisdom about fear and control when she said, **"When people believe that they have nothing, they are willing to give up everything to gain something."**

After all the pain and loss these individuals had caused others, this woman could still acknowledge their collective pain behind their violent fight to take back control of their lives.

The need to feel in control is so strong that some people will even sabotage their own lives in an attempt to keep control. For example, believing that they will *always* fail – regardless of what they do – some people decide to take control by "choosing" to fail. For example, a student may decide to not turn in his homework anymore. Or an employee, after being warned, may continue to arrive late to work every day. In both of these cases, a person sabotages his life in order to feed his belief of being a failure. They both believe they are victims.

Four Reasons People Choose to Fail

I believe there are four reasons people choose to fail. All four reasons are based on their fear of loss of control and the need to keep some form of control over their lives.

1. **Fear of not always measuring up to other people's expectations**
   These people are terrified of being judged. They often appear to be lazy or are procrastinators.

2. **Fear of incompetence**
   These people are afraid they don't have the ability to do

well. They feel they can't live with themselves if they don't succeed. If they do just enough to get by, they can always say they didn't give it their best.

3. **Fear of experiencing failure**
   These people want to feel safe. They insulate themselves from fear and pain by using control. They will often blame others or put up a protective wall to keep you out, saying things like, "You can't make me succeed. This is stupid. I don't need to prove I can do this."

4. **Fear that they are a failure**
   These people are afraid – and believe deep down inside – that they are failures. To maintain this belief, they need to convince others that they are right about being a failure. You may hear them say, "See, I told you I couldn't do it. I told you I'd fail."

Facing Fear

Fear is based on the belief that, in some way, you are not enough. You create fear whenever you feel your control is being taken away. When you lose control, you try to become a controller, so it is important for you to know what triggers fear in you.

Remember, your reactive brain is in control when you are in fear mode; you automatically go into a "fight or flight" pattern. To get out of your fear, you must first admit that you are afraid and validate your feelings. After you acknowledge your fear, you can process it through your higher-level brain functions. Once you understand your reactions to fear and know you are good enough, you don't need to try to control and take power from others.

Reconnecting With Ourselves

Behind every bully's or victim's mask are many wounds

caused by emotional or physical pain coming from some type of loss. The deeper the wound, the stronger the belief in being powerless.

To regain balance after a loss, we need to find something to replace what we have lost. But first, **the most important thing we have to rediscover is our *Self* – the core of who we are as a person.**

After we reconnect with our Self, we need to feed ourselves with positive self-talk. Instead of putting ourselves down, we need to say encouraging words like:

"That's okay; I'll do better next time."

Or . . .

"I'm not stupid; I just have to learn it my way."

The Bully & Victim Dance. It always begins when we believe that, in some way, we are not good enough. This negative belief triggers fear, and the reactive brain immediately prepares the body for fight or flight. This negative belief also serves as the catalyst for the creation of a mask.

When our body is in fight or flight mode, our fear causes us to become a controller. This is when we choose to create and wear either the bully or the victim mask by using one or more of the four techniques for taking control. Bullies choose to "fight." Victims choose "flight," hoping to escape their fear by being saved by a stronger person.

The first step to taking off the bully or victim mask is to admit that you're wearing the mask. Bullies need to identify and own their true identity by *understanding* instead of *judging* themselves. Only then will they see how their fears of not being enough and feeling powerless are connected to their need for power and control. Victims need to *admit* that they believe they are powerless and that they *choose* to give away their power in order to survive. When they see how their fears of not being enough are connected to their need to give away their power, they can begin to take back true control of their lives.

> We are all capable of putting on a mask that helps to disguise the battle of fear being fought inside us. The person behind the mask is someone who fears losing control and hungers to know that he or she is enough.

Using Education to Heal

If we want to stop children from creating bully masks, our educational system needs to offer all students classes in conflict resolution, anger management, and emotional literacy using age-appropriate materials. After students understand that bullies are actually weak and afraid (even though they may come across as tough and strong), they probably will not want to become known as bullies themselves.

There are many reasons that people become bullies, and they may need help uncovering and revealing the reasons behind their mask. Since most masks are created in childhood, we need to offer programs that give bullies in school the time and space to own and process their built-up anger. All bullies need a safe place to take off their masks and acquire greater self-awareness so they can heal their inner pain. If we continue to just punish bullies without helping them to process the reasons behind their anger, we will continue to see older bullies using greater acts of violence.

One program that can help bullies and their victims heal is the Restorative Justice Program. If you are interested in learning more about this program, please refer to Appendix 10 in this book.

In the next chapter you will discover how the fear of not being enough carries over into our adult lives.

If you want to move your greatest obstacle, realize
that the obstacle is yourself
– and that the time to act is now!

Nido Qubein

CHAPTER NINE

THE ADULT BULLY

The memory of a controlling parent who yelled at you and belittled you for spilling soda when you were 10 years old can rear its ugly head when your own son spills his soda in the living room. Without realizing it, you can become your mother or father scolding you when you were a child. This type of memory can also be triggered at work whenever a boss or employee belittles a co-worker for making a mistake.

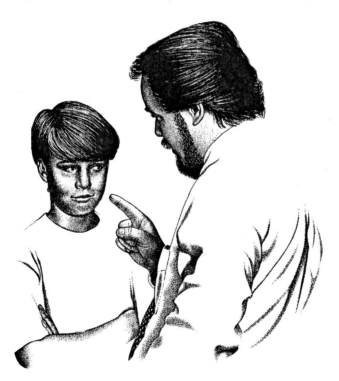

Another common scenario occurs when a teenager rolls his or her eyes and responds to an adult's comment with,

"Whatever!" This comment often triggers adults into feeling that they're not being respected. Within a millisecond, the adult's mind reviews their fear of loss of power and finds the justification for taking back control.

"I'm being disrespected... which means I'm not being treated like I'm a good enough parent. My child isn't respecting me. I have to take back control. I have to get back their respect by showing them that I'm the one in control, and I'm good enough to be respected."

The parent then becomes a controller by using one of the four control techniques. The deeper the trigger of not feeling good enough, the more aggressive will be the technique that parent uses to try to control the child. Child abuse is often the result of this triggered reaction.

Parents can chuckle about their over-reactive punishments-- "You are grounded for a month... a year... the rest of your life!"-- long after the moment of anger has passed. However, in the workplace an angry boss may say, "You're fired!" to an employee who unknowingly crossed the line, even if that employee has a good work record.

We all can experience fear inside us whenever we don't feel like we're enough. With the right trigger, we can all "lose our cool," feel out of control, and turn into controllers.

Dusting Off Our Childhood Masks

A mask can be dusted off and used over and over again until the person behind the mask outgrows his/her need to use it. As you already know, adults who choose to wear the mask in the workplace are still living by old belief patterns formed in childhood. The more deeply their trigger is related to fear of losing control, the faster they try to become a controller.

Aggressive Controllers

Whenever adults recall negative judgments or control techniques that were inflicted on them in childhood, the memories can trigger fears of reliving the pain and the shame connected to those experiences. The greater the amount of emotional and or physical pain connected to the memory, the faster they lash out at other people. (See "Four Ways We Try to Control Others" in Chapter Three). This act of lashing out usually occurs whenever they believe their self-worth is being threatened, such as when they feel they are being disrespected by a co-worker or peer.

A boss or employee who belittles a co-worker may feel overwhelmed, inadequate, or terrified of losing control in some or all parts of his/her life. Many adults who haven't worked through their negative beliefs from childhood will often carry their beliefs into situations where they feel they'll lose (or have lost) control. Feeling threatened, they will usually become controllers.

For example, the belief "If I don't have control, I might get hurt," might develop because a child learned that he couldn't trust adults to keep him safe. Perhaps he had a controlling parent who physically abused him, and he promised himself that he would never let another person hurt him again. So in order to be safe, he now has to always be the one in control.

When this happens, a child may grow up to be a very controlling boss who belittles his employees. Since he believes that he can't trust people, he can never let his guard down and be their friend. He believes that he has to be in total control at all times to feel safe at work. His lack of trust and his fear of losing control serve as the basis for his bully mask.

Passive-Aggressive Controllers

The fear of loss of control can also come in the guise of a "pleaser." For example, a little girl developed the belief, "In order for me to be loved and survive, I have to please people." Pleasers choose to give up their Self in order to survive. As an adult, this little girl continued to use her ability to please others in order to control them. She used generosity with strings attached. However, if her gifts or favors weren't reciprocated by her employees and friends the way she expected them to be, she became angry and took back what she so generously gave away. As a result, the recipients of her gifts and favors often ended up owing her for her generosity!

This type of scenario is often seen in elementary schools when children bring candy to school to impress their peers. They, too, have a motive behind their gifts: to be liked and accepted by everyone.

Here is an example of a passive-aggressive controller, a "pleaser" who used generosity in the workplace to control others.

THE "PLEASER"

Every morning, a warm, sweet, friendly woman came into the office and gave each of the other employees hugs, wonderful compliments, baked goods, flowers, and other gifts. She made them all feel wonderful, and they loved how positive and friendly she was every morning.

However, the rest of the day she spent behind a closed door talking on the phone to her friends, reading magazines, and doing very little work. Eventually, her co-workers took it on themselves to finish her work so they could complete what needed to get done before the end of the day.

As a consultant for the company, I met with the employees and saw the woman's game. I explained to them that she was controlling them with her sweetness and disarming them every morning by being so kind and generous. Until then, no one wanted to confront her about her work because they feared they might hurt her feelings. After they realized how she was playing the pleaser role in order to control them, they decided it was time to confront her and not feel guilty about hurting her feelings. For years, this woman had orchestrated her life around pleasing other people in order keep control. She had learned this technique from her alcoholic mother.

When we are healthy and balanced, acts of giving and receiving are the same; both are based upon love. But when we are emotionally unhealthy, we may give with strings attached for a desired outcome. Or we may turn the act of receiving into taking things away from others in order to control them.

Both giving and receiving, when performed in an unhealthy way, are based upon fear. Whenever we focus on our fears, we put our energy into what we fear and create more loss for ourselves and for those we work and live with. Therefore, the more we fear loss, the more we set ourselves up to lose.

Reminder

Whenever people are wearing masks we need to:

- Validate their fears.
- Look for their fears and the control techniques they are using.
- Discover what they are gaining by using those control techniques.
- Consider what beliefs could be behind their fears.
- Identify their beliefs, and try to understand how to help them eliminate or work through their fears.

The next chapter offers suggestions for dealing with a bully in many areas of life. Take your newfound understanding of why a person becomes a bully and apply it in the following chapter.

In this life we will encounter hurts and trials that we will not be able to change; we are just going to have to allow them to change us.

Ron Lee Davis

CHAPTER TEN

WHAT DO YOU DO WITH A BULLY?

No one should knowingly allow another person to be threatened by a bully. Also, everyone needs to have a plan for dealing with a bully. Now that you understand how and why a person wears the bully mask, it's time to become proactive and be prepared to deal with any bully in your life.

Right now there are too many children and adults experiencing the pain and shame of being bullied. These people need a great deal of empathy and compassion from their families, friends, and co-workers to help them cope. We also need to remember that bullies are created from their own inner pain and fear. Therefore, even though they may appear to us to be unapproachable, they still need our help and understanding. The following pages contain action plans for successfully working with and disarming the bullies in our homes, our schools, and our businesses.

When a person is bullied, it is everyone's responsibility to help stop the bully.

FOR STUDENTS

What to Do if Your Friends or Peers are Bullying You

- Don't join the Bully & Victim Dance. STOP and think!

- Don't let the bully take your energy.

- Remember: only a weak person feels powerless and needs to take another person's power.

- Identify why you were selected. Why does the bully see you as a good victim?

- Accept the fact that the bully sees you as someone who will give his/her power away.

- Reread the victim quiz in Chapter Seven. Notice which items on the list you say "yes" to.

- Decide to not give the bully your power by letting the bully hurt or control you.

- Tell someone who can help change the situation: a friend, a teacher, a parent, a principal, a counselor, a bus driver, a minister, anyone you trust.

- Ask someone with the authority to move you to a different space away from the bully (such as your locker, or your seat on the bus or in the classroom).

- Try not to react. The bully wants to see that you're afraid or hurt.

- Ignore the bully. By not giving the bully your power, the bully usually looks for another victim.

- Keep a record of when and how the bully tried to hurt you.

Unmasking Bullies

- Remain calm and remember that the only reason people put you down is to put themselves up. People can't make you mad unless you choose to let them.

- Since you were selected to be bullied, learn from the experience and choose to see yourself as a stronger person from now on.

What to Do if You See Someone Being Bullied

When you become aware that someone is being bullied, you have the responsibility to help that person. However, in some cases, it may be best not to directly handle the bully by yourself. So what can you do?

- Don't just ignore the situation, hoping it will stop. It probably won't, and the person being bullied needs some support.

- Do not encourage the bully by laughing or making fun of the person being bullied.

- Help the person being bullied by sticking up for him/her. Invite that person to walk with you or sit next to you.

- Tell the bully to stop.

- Tell a teacher or some other responsible adult nearby what is going on.

If the bully is physically hurting someone, or if you are alone and not a match for the bully:

- Go find help right away.

- Startle the bully and attract the attention of others by making a loud noise (yell, honk your car horn, slam your locker door, etc.).

FOR PARENTS

What to Do When You See Your Child Putting on the Bully Mask

- Acknowledge that your child is acting like a bully out of fear.

- Identify the fear trigger; discover the fear behind the bullying behavior.

- Identify what your child is trying to gain from the negative behavior.

- Identify the belief behind his/her fear.

- Help your child admit and face his/her fear.

- Consider whether you or other family members are contributing to the fear.

- Speak to your child while you're doing a task together (working on a puzzle, loading the dishwasher, walking the dog, etc.).

- Validate the fear. For example, state to your child:
  - "You are very angry, and I want to understand how I can help you."
  - "There's something bothering you that we'll work out together."

- Depending on your child's age, explain what you know about bullies.

- Make the comparison to animals puffing up to scare predators away when they're afraid – just like we do by strutting and acting "cool."

- Keep your voice calm, yet be firm and strong.

- Use simple statements.

- Listen to what your child says.

- Help your child understand the following: "The only reason we put others down is to put ourselves up."

- Help your child understand that you love him/her unconditionally, but you don't like the negative behavior.

- Discuss plans for restitution to any victims.

- Discuss punishment. Include steps for resolving the fear that will change the negative behavior.

- Get a tutor to help your child if he/she is struggling in school.

- Talk to professionals for support, and address any physical or emotional abuse problems.

- Meet with the child's counselor, teachers, and principal to have a team approach for helping your child.

- Create balance in your child's life by including or adding some activity that will boost his/her self-esteem.

- Continue to monitor your child's behavior.

What to Do When Your Child is Bullied

No child should be bullied. If your child can't stop the bully alone, you may need to help. Whether your child is being bullied by one person or a group, it can be very painful. Sit down with your child and go over the information in this book, making it age-appropriate for them to understand. Look over the following list of suggestions and use the ones that apply to your child.

- Talk with your child's teacher or principal and have them help you by enforcing a "no bully tolerance policy" in their school.

- Explain to your child that kids who bully others are looking for someone they can easily dominate because they need to feel like they are in control and more powerful.

- Explain to your child that bullies think nice kids are a good target, choosing to bully and tease them because they're too "nice" to fight back.

- Tell your (older) child that he/she really has the power, that bullies really feel powerless. Your child can choose to keep his/her power by not letting the bully push their buttons. Help your child understand why bullies put other people down.

- "Divide and conquer" a group of bullies. Bullies are really cowards. Have your (older) child talk to each of the bullies separately and tell them to stop bothering him/her. Have your child encourage friends to help him/her speak to the bullies.

- Talk to the bully or the bully's parents. It may be best to have your child handle the bully alone, without your direct and obvious help. (Kids can be cruel and may call a child "mama's boy or girl" if a parent gets involved). However, if your child can't talk to them, you can talk to each child separately or to their parents.

FOR TEACHERS

What to Do With a Bully in Your Classroom

Obviously, teenage bullies are bigger, stronger, and harder to manage than elementary students – especially if they are angry. Use your discretion and devise a plan that works for you. The following list contains some points and suggestions for you to consider when making up your own classroom management plan:

- Understand instead of judging the behavior. Remember, bullies would rather look "bad" than "stupid" to their classmates.

- Keep a written record of each incident.

- Look over your notes to find out when the student acts out the most. See if there is a pattern to the triggers for the negative behavior.

- See if you can identify what the student is gaining by his/her behavior.

- Identify the fear going on in the classroom or in their life. They will want to get out of class if they feel threatened or uncomfortable.

- Include some type of movement to diffuse their anxiety. "Okay class, let's take a two-minute break to stand up and stretch."

- Validate the student's fear and anger, and ask how you can help. "I can tell you're uncomfortable with this. How can I help you feel better?" (This is said quietly and not in front of the other students.)

- Help these students find balance between what they like to do and what they believe they aren't good at doing. Include what they like to do in your classroom.

- Change the routine. "I know that we've been sitting for a long time. Why don't we all stand up and . . .?"

- Divert the bully's power-taking techniques with a different teaching approach by using age-appropriate humor and creativity to catch the bully off-guard. For example:

  - "I'm sorry. I'm losing some of you. Perhaps I need to say it another way." Then proceed to speak in a regional or foreign accent.

  - Tell your students to close their eyes and to listen very carefully to what you say. Then when they know an answer, they should raise their hand.

  - Take your class on a mental journey where they can experience your lesson. For example, take your class to a medieval town or have them experience a colorful chapter from one of the books they are reading. This technique is great for social studies, science, history, and language arts.

- Depending on the circumstance and the age of the student, involve him/her in a directed activity – pass out papers, sharpen pencils, fix the calendar, put up art pictures, collect books, water the plants, etc.

- Use the spotlight in a positive way. "Why don't you come up and assist me by . . . ?"

- Ask the bully to perform a task that you know he/she can do well.

- Stay calm; respond to their negative comments and attitude with a simple, controlled response.

- Imply to the student that he/she has a need to resolve. "Are you feeling okay today? I believe that you're trying to tell me something." (This is said quietly to the student, not in front of the class.)

- Discuss the situation with your principal or school counselor.

If the student continues the behavior . . .

Call the student out into the hall and make your power statement. "Your behavior is unacceptable. If you chose to continue this behavior, you'll be sent to the office. Do you understand?"

Or if you already gave the student a warning through verbal or eye contact, and you feel he/she doesn't need to be given a second chance:

- Have your student take a seat at the back or outside the classroom. Give him/her a book that involves various topics of interest that you have ready for such occasions. Have the student read it and copy some passages by hand. Then have the student write his/her thoughts about what they learned from the material.

- If you feel you need to remove the student from the classroom, you can also have him/her sit in the back of another teacher's class and copy a book or some worksheets. Some teachers set this up ahead of time to help each other. This is usually done in a team-teaching situation when they both know the student.

- Depending on the age of the student, accompany him/her to the office, or notify the office that you're sending the student to the office.

Speaking Alone With the Student

- If possible, work on a task together while you discuss his/her behavior. Many students are more capable of verbally expressing and organizing their thoughts when this is combined with movement. This is especially true when they have to talk about their emotions.

- Discuss the student's behavior, and set up your statements so that he/she has to explain their actions or comments to you. Examples:
  - "I want to make sure that I heard you correctly . . . "
  - "I want to understand why . . ."
  - "What is it you can tell me so I can understand your reason for . . . ?"

- Explain to the student: For every action we choose, there's a reason for the choice. Negative actions are caused by negative thoughts. Negative thoughts are usually connected to fear. Talk with the student about his/her fear.

- Use play-acting to mimic the student's behavior before discussing his/her negative actions. You can say, "I want you to watch me and tell me what you think about my actions." Then ask:
  - "What did I look like when I acted like . . . ?"
  - "What did I sound like when I said . . . ?"

Never!

- Get into a confrontation in front of the class.
- Argue with the student.
- Plead with the student to behave.
- Let the student cause you to change your plan. (*You* have the choice.)
- Respond to the student out of negative emotion.
- Join the bully's dance.

Unmasking Bullies 97

If you lose control, don't beat yourself up. Tomorrow is a new day!

Quick Action Plan for Managing a Classroom Bully

Make sure your students know your classroom rules at the beginning of each semester or school year. However, when a bully acts out in your classroom:

- Do not draw attention to the bully.

- Take time to assess the student's gain and the trigger for his/her behavior. (Do this only if you perceive there is no danger to your students or to you.)

- Eliminate the trigger if possible.

Or . . .

- Take the focus off the student by using a movement activity or some type of diversion with the whole class involved.

- Involve the student in your lesson.

- Work at keeping the student in your class unless the other students are being affected.

Remember, the bully's goal is to get out of your classroom if he/she feels powerless. In order to feel safe in a threatening situation, we all need an escape plan. I've worked with classroom bullies who have shared their lists of what they can do to get out of certain classes whenever they feel uncomfortable. They know which button to push for each teacher. They make it a point to study you – it is how they have learned to survive!

Perhaps you've noticed that some students act up a lot more with a substitute teacher. Many bullies do not feel safe with a substitute teacher because the substitute may put them in a situation where they feel out of control. (They can't control what they don't know.) Believing that it's better to look bad rather than stupid to their peers, they will disrupt a substitute's classroom as fast as they can in order to be kicked out of a very uncomfortable situation. That way they can feel safe and in control of the situation.

FOR FAMILY AND FRIENDS

How to Handle a Bully in Your Home

Decide to take action NOW by taking control of your life.

- If the bully is physically, sexually, or emotionally abusive, tell someone you can trust. Leave and get to safety.

- Seek help from a family member, counselor, teacher, principal, minister, or agency (YWCA, YMCA, United Way).

- Consider that the bully in your home may need to be helped by a professional person.

- Realize that you don't have to live in fear. With help, a bully can be stopped.

- Decide not to allow a family member to bully you.

- Know that it won't get better until you decide to stop giving your power away.

- Remember that you are enough and you don't deserve to be bullied.

- Ask yourself why you're being bullied.

- Try to understand how the bully is using you.

- Keep track of how and when the bully is abusive.

- See if you can discover what belief is feeding the bully's fear.

- Speak up for yourself. You are worth it!

- Try not to feed the bully by joining his/her dance.

FOR CO-WORKERS

Techniques the Workplace Bully Uses

Remember: all anger is based on a fear of not being enough. The workplace bully will use many masks and techniques to take control or power from others.

- Overloads you with work
- Disarms you using guilt
- Ridicules you
- Ignores you
- Physically or emotionally threatens or hurts you
- Badmouths you
- Uses generosity to control you or others

How to Handle a Workplace Bully

Ignore the bully's behavior while you assess it. Then use one or more of the ideas from this list to deal with the situation.

- Share and discuss your concerns with a friend or professional.

- Try to understand the reasons behind the bully's behavior.

- Identify the control technique. What is the bully's fear? (This will help you feel more confident about resolving the problem.)

- Acknowledge your part as the chosen victim.

- Review "Ways We Try to Control Others" in Chapter Three.

- Keep detailed records of each incident in case you need to prove the behavior.

- Contact or make an appointment with your department supervisor or the human resources director. Or if your workplace has an employee assistance program, you can contact that office.

- Confront the bully.

- Write a letter to the bully discussing his/her behavior and your reactions. Send a copy to someone who oversees your workplace.

Ask Yourself Before You Take on a Bully at Work:

- Will the management or administrative group support you?

- Will the person in authority choose to be responsible enough to carry out the necessary restrictions or confrontation?

- Are you likely to lose your job over this?

- What impact will fighting the bully have on your personal life (family, health, friends, co-workers)?

- Do you plan to remain at this job if you lose?

- How much are you willing to give up in order to gain?

- Can you transfer to another part of the company? To a different building?

- Can you avoid further contact with the bully?

- Will you still look forward to going to work?

- Will the bully continue to influence your position at work if you stay?

How to Cope

- Become the observer, not the judge.

- Stay as detached, patient, and alert as you can.

- Do physical workouts to release your pent-up anger, such as yoga, jogging, or swimming.
- Listen to peaceful music.
- Write down your feelings.
- Discuss your feelings with friends.
- Use humor.
- Focus on the good parts of your life, and stay balanced and focused.
- Keep your perspective – this, too, shall pass!

Take a long ride down a highway or country road with the windows rolled up. Scream and contort your face as much as you can. Get it out! Let out any sounds you've stifled inside or any words you've squelched. Really get into it! You'll feel so much better after you get your anger out. You may also choose to do this in an isolated place where you can park your car.

Think about the worst-case scenario. Will you survive it? This will give you inner strength because you'll have already thought through your worst fears! (Refer back to Chapter Seven.)

When a Bully Enters Your Life

- You have the opportunity to become stronger and wiser.
- You have the opportunity to change old victim patterns.
- You have the opportunity to learn how to stay in control.
- You have the opportunity to learn how to let go in order to gain.

Until you are willing to let go, you aren't ready to confront the bully. Just sensing your fear of loss gives the bully more power. When you can let go of what you fear you'll lose, you'll become stronger.

EPILOGUE

NOW THAT YOU KNOW!

When life gives us our biggest challenges, we take our biggest leaps of growth. What seems like the worst thing that can happen often serves as a catalyst to steer our lives in a more positive and fulfilling direction.

Perhaps we bring in adversity to create change in our lives. In any event, we know that pain always brings the opportunity for change. **When a bully enters your life, you have the opportunity to change your life and increase your self-worth.** Remember, bullies look for the weakest person to control.

As you witness yourself either wearing the bully mask or becoming the bully's victim, use the information presented in this book to become aware of the role you are choosing to play in the Bully & Victim Dance. Own your part in the role you've chosen to play, and look for the beliefs that support each participant's role in the dance. When you decide to let go of the belief that draws you into the dance, you'll stop performing the dance steps.

By sharing what you've learned about bullies and victims with other people, you can do your part to help this world become a safer and healthier place for everyone.

APPENDICES

Some of the information in this section also appears in the author's book, *Why Not You?*

APPENDIX 1

SELF-ESTEEM BUILDERS

For Bullies and Victims

- Smile when you see me.
- Call me by my name.
- Listen to what I say.
- Tell me that you missed me when I was absent.
- Recognize my special talents.
- Compliment me or notice when I do something right.
- If you don't like what I do, remind me that you still value me as a person.
- Expect me to succeed.
- Encourage me to succeed at the task I am given.
- Give me a chance to succeed in at least one small way every day.
- If you wish to correct me, take me aside and do it privately.

APPENDIX 2

QUOTES & WRITINGS TO PONDER

Worry is a misuse of imagination.
- Dan Zadra -

Any kid who has two parents who are interested in him and has a houseful of books isn't poor.
- Sam Levenson -

You have no idea what a poor opinion I have of myself – and how little I deserve it.
- W.S. Gilbert -

Self-knowledge is the beginning of self-improvement.
- Spanish Proverb -

An optimist may see a light where there is none, but why must the pessimist always run to blow it out?
- Michael De Saint Pierre -

He who has a why to live can bear almost any how.
- F. Nietzche -

I cannot give you the formula for success, but I can give you the formula for failure – which is try to please everybody.
- Herbert Bayard Swope -

There are two ways of spreading light: to be the candle, or the mirror that reflects it.
- Edith Wharton -

When a man blames others for his failures, it is a good idea to credit others with his success.
- Howard W. Newton -

To be wronged is nothing unless you continue to remember it.
- Confucius -

When you know you know, they know you know.
- Mary Louise Blakely -

APPENDIX 3

LETTING GO

To "let go" does not mean to stop caring. It means I can't do it for someone else.

To "let go" is not to cut myself off. It's the realization that I can't control another.

To "let go" is to admit powerlessness, which means the outcome is not in my hands.

To "let go" is not to try to change or blame another. It's to make the most of myself.

To "let go" is not to care for, but to care about.

To "let go" is not to fix, but to be supportive.

To "let go" is not to judge, but to allow another to be a human being.

To "let go" is not to be in the middle, arranging all the outcomes, but to allow others to affect their own destinies.

To "let go" is not to deny, but to accept.

To "let go" is not to nag, scold, or argue, but instead to search out my own shortcomings and correct them.

To "let go" is not to adjust everything to my desires, but to take each day as it comes and cherish myself in it.

To "let go" is not to regret the past, but grow and live for the future.

To "let go" is to fear less and love more.

- Author Unknown -

APPENDIX 4

HELPFUL MULTISENSORY TECHNIQUES FOR TEACHERS

- Left hemisphere-dominant learners are interested in ordered parts, process, and semantics. They need to see the details.

- Right hemisphere-dominant learners are interested in expression and the flow of language. They need to see the whole picture to answer their "Why?" questions.

Reading Techniques

- Teach students a question-and-answer reading technique. Show them how they can mentally turn all headings and subheadings into questions and then read the text that follows as answers to those questions.

- Use a green transparency over what is being read.

- Have students sit on large balls as they read. Bouncing, swaying, and rocking movements can increase focus and memory.

- Have students hold something in their hands when reading in order to help them stay focused on the material.

- Use phrase sheets to increase fluency. Challenge students to read all of the phrases within a certain amount of time. For example:
  - saw the dog
  - ran to the house
  - over the green river

- Have students read into a recorder to hear and correct their own mistakes. This helps them to become discerning readers.

- Have students walk and read at the same time. When students are afraid that they can't read, walking helps to take away the fear and unblocks their thought process. This technique increases fluency and comprehension.

- Have the students close their eyes and direct them to see pictures in their minds as you read to them. This helps visually unconscious students practice using their visual sense internally for comprehension; it will carry over as they read to themselves.

- Use web mapping for students to organize the events, characters, etc. of a story.

- Cut up cartoons and ask students to put them in the correct sequence. This helps visually unconscious students to understand cause and effect. It also helps right hemisphere-dominant students to organize their thoughts.

- Use color shock. Separate compound words or syllables by color instead of spaces. Right hemisphere-dominant students need to see the whole picture before they process the parts. Using spaces to separate the words into syllables can confuse them.

- Have students sing sentences. This helps visually and auditorily unconscious students to stay focused on the information.

- Have students use different voices as they read. Using a foreign or regional accent helps them to stay focused on the material they are reading. They can also become characters, reading with their voice changed to match how the character might sound. (Little children love to read as if they were a dinosaur reading out loud.)

- Have students clap, walk, hop, jump, etc. as they read each word in the sentence. This helps kinesthetic children to slow down their minds and see the word order in sentences.

- When teaching spelling or vocabulary, "write" the words on the students' backs.

- Have students act out what they read.

- Have students touch their fingers to what they are reading (e.g., books, tests, computer screens) as their eyes scan down the page. This is known as "grounding." It helps visually unconscious processors with their anxiety before they take a test or read some text.

- Have kinesthetically dominant students touch all pictures and imagine what it would be like to feel each part of the picture as if it were real. This helps with visual recall.

- Have students circle consonant blends (i.e., bl, fl, gr) or vowels in newspaper articles or magazines within a certain amount of time. This helps them to move their eyes across the page and teaches them to be more discerning about how words begin and end.

A final technique for developing reading skills is called the **Warning Game**. This game helps students become more aware of their lazy reading habits. It can be played with an entire class or in a tutoring situation.

Have students read a paragraph out loud. If they make a mistake, say "Warning" after they come to the end of the sentence in which the mistake was made. If the students can find their mistake, they get a point. If they can't, you get a point.

When using this game in a group, divide the group into two teams. As one student reads, the other students have to pay very close attention so that they can help their teammate if the student who is reading asks for assistance. The student who is reading can choose to find his/her mistake or ask a teammate for help. If the student or teammate fails to find the mistake, the other team gets a chance to answer. Whichever team finds the mistake gets the point.

Writing Techniques

- To teach writing to kinesthetic students, start with the large muscles first. Have them write large letters with their whole arm in the air, on a chalkboard, or on a large piece of paper as they close their eyes. It is important for them to have spatial awareness. Have them mimic the shape of letters with their bodies as they lay on the floor or stand up.

  Then have them make the same movements while their elbows are resting on the desk or floor. Have them write letters in the air. Continue to engage increasingly smaller muscles by using sand, paint, or a chalkboard. After they have good eye-hand control and spatial awareness, have them write on paper with a pencil.

- Use toothpaste to write letters or words on a table.

- Use sand or crushed noodles glued to paper in the shape of a letter. Have them close their eyes and trace the letters as they say the sounds.

Math Techniques

1) First explain what you are going to teach them and why.

2) Create an overall picture. Tell them that you will go through the entire math problem first so they can see what it looks like before you break it down.

3) Go through the entire problem as you say your steps and thoughts out loud.

4) Next, go over the same problem step-by-step with your students.

5) Give them time to write each step down.

6) Supply another similar math problem for them to work on with you and at their desks.

7) Have them say the steps out loud with you as they mimic your actions. Have them teach the problems back to each other in a buddy situation.

8) Review with another similar problem on the board or overhead, and encourage your students to complete the problem. Supply an example of a problem that they already completed.

Here are some other ideas.

- Take the numbers out of story problems. Have your students see the story first. Act out the story, if possible, or draw a picture.

- Use manipulatives to teach math concepts; anything that can be held in their hands can be used. Get your students out of their chairs so they can use their large muscles as much as possible. For example, if you are teaching place values, have your students stand up in a line and give them each a card with a number on it. See if they can get their bodies in the correct order when you give them a number verbally.

- Always use the teach-back approach to imprint your math lesson. Use charts and pictures as much as possible.

- Include large muscle movement, rhymes, raps, etc. to increase long-term recall.

- Have students jump and say math facts as they look at the factors. You can also use a trampoline, hula hoop, jump rope, or a cheerleader approach.

- Always include both the large and small muscles of the body. Be creative and make the lessons fun. This tends to be a scary subject for many visually and kinesthetically unconscious students.

Study Skills and Focusing

- Use lots of note cards in different colors. By using note cards and writing down key points from the information that they read, kinesthetic students who are visually unconscious will be able to study as they walk.

- Play Bach, Mozart, Beethoven, or Handel while they study. Certain kinds of Western classical music appear to increase the brain's ability to take in information.

- Allow students to take off their shoes. Kinesthetics seem to perform better on tests and stay focused longer on their work when their feet can feel the floor. Most of them take their shoes off as soon as they get home; it grounds them.

- Use a "Red Hot" folder for all assignment papers.
  - "Red Hot" means something is important and needs attention right away.
  - Visually unconscious students find notebooks with separate subject sections too confusing.
  - By using one folder, parents only have to check one place to see papers that are brought home.
  - It helps students to stop stuffing papers into books, where they usually get lost in the shuffle.
  - The folder should have a favorite design, sports team, music group, or hero on the cover. The more emotion that is attached to the folder, the better.

- Put the students who seem to have the hardest time staying focused on the aisle, where you can pat them on the back or touch their arms. They will come back from their daydreams when they are touched.

- Allow your kinesthetic students time to get drinks and move their large muscles. Some will perform better if they stand at a counter while they take tests.

- To help settle down young children, have them do somersaults or swing; do not have them spin.

- The Magic Lotion Technique is another good way to help little ones settle down. Have them pretend that they have a magic bottle of lotion that settles them down after they finish rubbing it all over their arms, legs, necks, and faces. This technique helps them to stimulate their neurological system in a controlled manner; it will calm them down.

- Encourage all of your students to drink water!!

Thinking Skills

- Have your students practice brain patterning exercises. An example of this is the command and repeat exercise. Tell the students a series of commands, then have them repeat those commands back to you exactly as you said them. If they say the commands correctly in the right order, they may perform the commands. For example, say, "Take three steps forward, turn left, put your left hand on your right hip, put your left hand on your right shoulder." Create longer and harder commands as they find the commands easier to master. This is an excellent exercise for all students who are struggling with their academic skills.

- Have students draw symmetrical pictures with each hand

at the same time. Then have them draw asymmetrical pictures with each hand at the same time.

- Have students draw one picture with their left hand and another picture with their right hand at the same time.

- Have students draw a picture with their right hand and write a sentence with their left hand at the same time.

For All Subjects and Learning Environments

- Use kinesthetic, visual, and auditory techniques, including color, emotion, and movement in your lessons.

- Get your students up and moving every 15 or 20 minutes. Allow them to have frequent drinks of water or water bottles in the classroom.

- Always include the teach-back approach or a demo to lock in the information.

- Supply projects and tests that offer students with each processing pattern the ability to show or express what they know.

- Allow gum chewing (preferably sugarless!) if possible. It involves jaw movement, which stimulates the brain. This helps kinesthetic students stay focused and is especially helpful during stressful activities, such as tests.

Communication Skills

- Remember: scared students would rather look "bad" than "stupid" to their peers. The more they strut, the greater their fear.

- A teacher who becomes a dictator or controller in order to maintain authority in his/her class will never actually have control.

- Students <u>want</u> to learn when they feel safe enough to risk.

- Teaching is the act of sharing your passion. Teachers don't turn the light on inside their students. They help their students discover the switch.

APPENDIX 5

HELPFUL MULTISENSORY TECHNIQUES FOR BUSINESSES

- Auditory processors need to say things out loud and teach back or demonstrate.

- Visual processors need to see charts, pictures, and color.

- Kinesthetic processors need to experience things through large and small muscle movements.

Include techniques that address all three processing styles – kinesthetic, visual, and auditory – as often as possible.

By incorporating the following suggestions throughout your business, you can meet every employee's needs.

- Post a visual flow chart that shows the relationship of all departments or work units and notes their tasks and responsibilities. This will help employees see the whole picture of the company and better understand and respect their position. (In a large company, many employees only know what their department does.)

- Post a visually interesting poster that describes the company's vision, mission, and goals.

- Use a teach-back approach and include kinesthetic techniques when training all employees.

- When tasks require small eye-hand movements or high stress, have employees take brief breaks every 20-30 minutes so they can relax their eyes from nearpoint focus.

- Allow employees to move and drink water at least every half hour.

- If possible, allow employees who choose to work to music to wear headphones.

- When training, break tasks down into parts. Make sure the employees understand the parts as well as the whole task.

- Do not assume that all employees can picture what is said. Visually unconscious processors may be reluctant to say that they don't understand something because they don't want to appear "stupid" in front of others.

- Use swivel chairs in meeting rooms for those who need to move to stay focused.

- Train the marketing staff to be familiar with all six processing patterns. This will help them learn how to approach and best serve each customer.

- Always use visuals and include some type of kinesthetic activity in your meetings. Some companies have discovered that placing skoosh balls on the table for kinesthetic employees is helpful.

- To make "reader friendly" written material, use a serif type face and large type. Break the material apart visually with spaces separating sections. Include visuals and color, such as line drawings, charts, graphs, and pictures.

- Have a visual agenda for any meeting, and go over it verbally before starting. This will help right hemispheric-dominant learners to feel less anxious and understand the whole picture.

- Use lightly colored green or yellow transparencies over computer screens to help employees' eyes.

- Offer both visual and auditory praise.

- Include the reasons for any changes in rules or procedures.

- Give employees time to figure numbers or compose written material. Never assume that an employee can add numbers or write what you need on the spot. (Even professional mathematicians and writers may not be able to produce "on the fly" if they are right-hemispheric dominant.)

Communication Skills

If you remember and practice the following ideas, you will go a long way toward creating a happier, healthier, more productive workplace.

- People who are truly in control see the value in all employees and do not need to act controlling in order to be in control.

- Praise publicly and correct privately.

- Where there is anger, there is fear. Where there is fear, discover the belief behind it and correct that.

- For a company to have success, it must see and treat every employee as an equally important part of the whole process. Lip-service to this idea is not enough.

- All company leaders need to promote and share their passion for the company's vision with all employees.

APPENDIX 6

EXERCISE 1
IDENTIFYING YOUR BELIEFS

Here is a paper-and-pencil exercise that can help you identify your core beliefs. Write down as a phrase or a sentence the first thought that comes into your mind. Don't judge your thought, just get it on paper. Then, at the end of that phrase, write the question, "Why?" Think about what the answer might be, write down that thought, and again put the question, "Why?" at the end of the phrase. Keep writing answers and asking yourself, "why" until you can't give another answer.

The series of statements below shows how this process works.

I am never organized. Why?
Everything is always a mess around me. Why?
I never have the time to pick things up. Why?
I'm too busy to be organized. Why?
I can't be both busy and organized. Why?
Because there's too much for me to handle. Why?
Because I'm always too busy to take care of things. Why?
Because I choose to be busy. Why?
Because I don't take time for myself. Why?
Because others come first. Why?
Because they are more important than I am. Why?
Because they count on me. Why?
Because I'm the only one that can be counted on. Why?

129

Because I never let anyone down. Why?
Because I don't want them to be upset with me. Why?
Because I want to keep everyone happy. Why?
Because then I feel good about myself. Why?
Because if I help people, I feel good. Why?
Because then I feel like I'm needed. Why?
Because I need to be needed. Why?
Because when I'm needed, I feel like I'm enough.

The core belief this exercise revealed is, "When I'm needed, I feel like I'm enough." This may seem to be totally unrelated to the first statement, "I am never organized," but the connection is clear once you've read the sequence of beliefs in between. Underneath each of your completed phrases is the motivating belief of that particular thought.

Now it's your turn to experiment with this discovery exercise. What do you believe when you are given the opening statement, "My life is . . ."? Turn to the next page.

Identifying Your Life Beliefs

Finish the statement, "My life is . . ." with whatever first comes to mind. Don't think about it too long. Answer the question, "Why?" with another statement. If you need more space, use additional pieces of paper. Keep going until you can't give another answer.

My life is

_____
Why?

_____
Why?

_____
Why?

_____
Why?

_____
Why?

_____
Why?

_____
Why?

_____
Why?

_____
Why?

_____ Why?

_____ Why?

_____ Why?

_____ Why?

_____ Why?

_____ Why?

_____ Why?

APPENDIX 7

EXERCISE 2
HOW WELL DO YOU NURTURE YOURSELF?

Take a piece of paper and cut a heart that is the size of your hand. As you read each question below, cut or tear off a piece of your heart that represents how much you feel you gave away during the past month.

- How often did you lose your temper?
- How often did you keep your mouth shut and not speak up for yourself?
- How much free time did you spend doing things for others?
- How much time did you spend solving another person's problems?
- How often did you skip a meal?
- How often did you do another person's job?
- How often did you stuff anger down inside yourself?
- How often did you go somewhere when you were sick and should have stayed home?
- How much junk food did you eat?
- How often did you tell yourself "no" when you could have said "yes"?

How much of your paper heart do you have left? Now, as you read each statement below, put back one or more pieces of the heart – enough to represent how much you gave to yourself this past month.

- Every time you said "No" to a person who asked for a favor.
- Every time you gave yourself some nurturing (hot-tub, music, flowers, book, exercise, etc.).
- Every time you spoke up for yourself.
- Every time you were able to delegate work rather than doing it yourself.
- Every time you played with friends.
- Every time you chose to eat healthy food.
- Every time you laughed.
- Every time you hugged someone.
- Every time you were alone and enjoyed yourself.

Do you have most of your heart put back together?

What did you discover by doing this exercise? How much of your heart did you give away? If you gave a lot, did you nurture yourself enough to stay balanced?

Think about what you can do to nurture yourself. When you give away too much of yourself, you can end up believing that people are just using you. This can lead to fear and anger. You may be afraid that there will be nothing left. Do you ask yourself, "But what about me?"

Of course, it is good to share and to help others, but not always at your own expense. If you have nothing left for yourself, then you have nothing more to give away. When you allow yourself to enjoy the abundance of life and share it with others, you create more abundance in your own life.

APPENDIX 8

EXERCISE 3
IDENTIFYING CLOSE ENERGY-TAKERS

Get a piece of paper and trace around your hand. You are going to label each finger with the initials of the four people who are your current closest relationships. First, put your own initials in the middle finger. Then, on either side of that finger, place the initials of the two people whom you consider to be closest to you.

Now, as you read each of the following 17 statements, decide which person best fits each one. Write an "X" on the finger representing that person. A statement may not seem to apply to any of the people you've selected, or you may feel that a statement fits two people equally well. Try to select the one person who fits the statement best, and you will end up with a total of 17 "X" marks scattered somewhere on the fingers.

- The person who is most like you.
- The person who has the same values as you.
- The person you most trust to keep a secret.
- The person you feel shares the most with you.
- The person whose lifestyle is most like yours.
- The person with whom you've had the most fun.
- The persons who hugs you the most.
- The person you can count on the most.
- The person who doesn't criticize you.
- The person you consider to be the most positive.

135

- The person who laughs with you the most.
- The person you think takes best care of himself/herself.
- The person who listens to you the most.
- The person who talks the least about other people's problems.
- The person who always makes you feel good.
- The person who is the most active.
- The person who has the most hopes and dreams.

Next, place an "0" on the appropriate finger for the person who best matches each of the following statements. You will end up with 17 "0" marks scattered among the fingers.

- The person who has the worst health.
- The person who is the unhappiest.
- The person who smokes or drinks the most.
- The person who worries the most.
- The person who is sick most often.
- The person who complains the most.
- The person who hangs on you the most.
- The person who has had the most loss in his/her life.
- The person who gets angry most often.
- The person who tells you the most about his/her problems.
- The person who has let you down the most.
- The person who makes the worst choices in friends or mates.
- The person who borrows from you most often.
- The person who most frequently expects the worst.
- The person who is the most stubborn.
- The person who most often puts others down.
- The person who never seems to be happy with life.

How to Interpret Your Results

To identify your energy takers, add up the amount of "X"s and "O"s on each finger. The people represented by the fingers with the largest number of "X"s give you the most energy. The people represented by the fingers with the largest number of "O"s take your energy.

Look at the pattern of "X"s and "O"s.

- Are both marks fairly evenly spread among the four people?

- Do you have one finger with a lot of both "X"s and "O"s? A finger with few of either?

- Did you put any "X"s or "O"s on the finger representing yourself? (Aren't you your own best friend?)

- Most important, do you have an energy taker next to your middle finger? If so, why do you spend so much time with this person? How can you stop him/her from taking your energy? Why do you give your energy to this person? Does this say something about your overall relationship with him/her?

APPENDIX 9

FOR FURTHER READING

Burns, David, M.D., *Ten Days to Self-Esteem*, New York: William Morrow & Sons, 1993.

Elgin, Suzette Harding, Ph.D., *You Can't Say That To Me! Stopping the Pain of Verbal Abuse-an 8 Step Program*, New York: Wiley and Sons, 1995.

Evans, Patricia, *The Verbally Abusive Relationship*, Holbrook, MA: Bob Adams, Inc. 1992.

Field, Tim, *Bully in sight: How to predict, resist, challenge and combat workplace bullying*, UK: Success Unlimited, 1996 (www.bullyonline.org)

Forward, Dr. Susan, Buck, Craig, *Toxic Parents-Overcoming Their Hurtful Legacy and Reclaiming Your Life*, New York: Bantam Books, 1989.

Jampolsky, Gerald G., M.D., *Love Is Letting Go Of Fear*, Berkley, CA: Celestial Arts, 1995.

Jeffers, Susan, *Feel the Fear and Do It Anyway*, New York: Ballantine Books, 1987.

Kline, Peter, *The Everyday Genius*, V.A.: Great Ocean Publishers, 1988.

Markova, Dawna, *How Your Child Is Smart*, Berkeley, CA: Comari Press, 1995.

Mitchell, W., *It's Not What Happens To You, It's What You Do About It*,
Denver, CO, Phoenix Press, 2001. Mitchell@WMitchel.com

Redfield, James, *The Celestine Prophecy*, New York, Warner Books, 1994.

Robbins, Anthony, *Notes from a Friend, A Quick and Simple Guide To Taking Control of Your Life*, New York: Simon & Schuster, 1995.

APPENDIX 10

THE RESTORATIVE JUSTICE PROGRAM

I believe that the Restorative Justice Program needs to be implemented in every school system and business where a positive approach to conflict resolution is sought. Since this book is about ways to understand and help bullies and victims, here is a brief explanation of the Restorative Justice Program.

Punishment for misbehavior may unintentionally encourage those who are punished (students and employees) to feel even more stigmatized and defiant. Suspensions and other exclusionary sanctions result in lost instruction or work time, which usually leads to increased failure. Often, those who are punished are not provided with the opportunity to fully understand how their behavior has affected other people. Thus, they view themselves as the victims. They are often repeat offenders who eventually drop out of school or quit work after being punished.

For school students, suspensions are often viewed as rewards (time off from school) or as a form of pride and prestige among their peer groups. Since current disciplinary procedures often ignore the needs of victimized students, they may inadvertently contribute to social withdrawal, learning disruption, or inappropriate retaliation.

The Restorative Justice Program is an alternative to current traditional disciplinary policies and procedures. It involves a process known as "conferencing." Conferencing is a process that deals with conflict within a group of people. Everyone affected by the conflict is invited to attend the conference and have any issues they raise adequately deliberated. A trained conference facilitator brings the group together and guides them through a collective examination of what has happened, how people have been affected, and what now needs to be done to make things better. A well-prepared and facilitated conference, led by a trained facilitator, allows the group to gain a shared understanding of the conflict and to begin to transform the conflict into understanding and cooperation.

This process has been used successfully in families and schools, the criminal legal system, in the workplace, in neighborhoods, and in local communities.

For more information contact:
Charles Wilson at wilchase@juno.com
P.O. Box 19361
Kalamazoo, MI 49019
Phone: 269-388-5899

APPENDIX 11

OTHER PUBLICATIONS BY MARY LOUISE BLAKELY

Why Not You?

A book that will help you understand why you do what you do.
Learn how you can take charge of your life!

Have you ever wondered . . .

Why do I seem to be going nowhere in my life?
Why am I so disorganized?
Why can't I find the right partner?
Why am I always angry?
Why do I always have to do everything for everyone else?
Why does my life feel like a soap opera?
WHY ME?

Whether you are a teacher, a parent, a student, an employee, a business owner, or a retiree, this book has answers that could change your life!

Praise for *Why Not You?* . . .

"Ask any CEO what their biggest business challenge is, and they will tell you it's *communication*. This book and Mary's training programs can help your company end its communication problems once and for all . . ."
Charlie Wicks, CEO & President, Pro Co Sound, Inc.

"A 'must read' for all parents and educators! Truly effective teachers must first know themselves and then their students."
Bill McNulty, 1998 Michigan Middle School Principal of the Year

"Mary is a most valuable referral source for my practice . . . She has incorporated her wealth of knowledge and years of experience into this book."
Ennis Berker, Ph.D., Neuropsychologist

"All hospitals need to hand this book out to every new parent!"
S. Bloomfield, Parent & Business owner

Math Rap Pak CD

Multiplication, Addition, Subtraction & Division facts on one CD!

Written and produced by Mary Louise Blakely. Music by Brian Drews and Brown & Brown Recording & Music Productions.

The *Math Rap Pak* helps all children and adults learn their math facts. This CD is especially helpful for predominantly kinesthetic processors, who need to move to retain information.

Each section of the CD introduces four areas of math facts by using a catchy rap beat with sports themes and various movements that encourage listeners to slap, clap, and shake their bodies while they learn their facts. Nationally acclaimed as one of the best math CDs for ADD & ADHD students, the *Math Rap Pak* is used in many schools and homes throughout the United States.

To order *Why Not You?* or the *Math Rap Pak*

Visit our Web page at: www.azuray.com

Or contact:

Azuray Learning, Inc.
P.O. Box 1748
Portage, MI 49081
Phone: 269-1877-974-SELF or 269-323-9280

APPENDIX 12

AZURAY LEARNING, INC.

Through Azuray Learning, Inc., Mary Louise Blakely offers a wide range of educational and personal development programs for teachers, parents, students, business people, and the general public. Some of these are listed here. For details and more information, visit our home on the World Wide Web at:

www.azuray.com
Or call toll-free
877-974-SELF

Seminars, Conferences, and Lectures

Based on the author's books: *Why Not You?* and *Unmasking Bullies & Victims*

For Education

- Creating a Classroom Environment Conducive to Each Student's Learning Pattern

- Why Smart Kids Fail and How To Help Them Succeed

- Communication Skills to Reduce Conflicts and Promote Learning and Teamwork in the School Environment.

- Unmasking Bullies & Victims – A Guide to Their Physiological, Psychological, and Emotional Patterns

For Business

- Understanding the Workplace Bully's Physiological, Psychological, and Emotional Patterns – How to Disarm and Work With the Power-Takers

- Communication Skills to Reduce Conflicts and Increase Productivity

- Sell to Your Customer's Thinking Pattern and Increase Your Sales

- Train Your Employees According to Their Learning Styles

- Understanding Entrepreneurs and How to Help Them Succeed

- Creating And Working Your Success Plan

For the General Public

Customized lectures and classes are available for individuals and groups that want to get the most out of the concepts discussed in the author's books.

Evaluation, Coaching, and Consulting Services

All services can be conducted on site, at Azuray's office, or on the telephone.

- Individual consulting services to assist in emotional, mental, and physical growth.

- Learning evaluations/consultations are available for individuals, families, groups, businesses, and other organizations.

Please refer to our Web page at www.azuray.com

Azuray Learning, Inc.
P.O. Box 1748
Portage, MI 49081
Phone: 269-323-9280

Or

1-877-974-SELF
E-mail: learning@azuray.com
www.azuray.com

ABOUT THE AUTHOR

Mary Louise Blakely is the president and CEO of Azuray Learning, Inc., a company that creates, produces, and markets multisensory learning tools and programs for children and adults. Azuray Learning is based in Kalamazoo, Michigan. Mary Louise is an educator, learning and behavior specialist, stress counselor, personal achievement coach, educational consultant, author, professional speaker, national radio talk-show personality, and clinical master hypnotherapist.

With degrees in education and psychology, and years of teaching in public schools and college classrooms, Mary Louise has devoted more than 20 years to teaching and creating educational and personal development achievement programs for children and adults. She is known as an expert in understanding, motivating, and assisting individuals and organizations in creating and implementing positive growth processes for success. Her expertise takes her into schools, colleges, and corporations across the country, where she offers training seminars, classes, lectures, and individual and group consultations.

Mary Louise specializes in multisensory learning and training techniques, conflict resolution, teamwork development, interpersonal communication, and the enhancement of personal potential. Her passion is to share her knowledge and experience by bringing awareness to those who seek greater success.

Printed in the United States
22738LVS00004B/403